COMPUTER ASSISTED PLANNING
OF
CURRICULUM AND INSTRUCTION

COMPUTER ASSISTED PLANNING
OF
CURRICULUM AND INSTRUCTION

*How to Use Computer-Based Resource Units
to Individualize Instruction*

James E. Eisele
University of Georgia

with

Gordon B. Bianchi
Bruce D. Burr
Thomas J. Clayback
Kenneth A. Cross

Educational Technology Publications
Englewood Cliffs, New Jersey 07632

Library of Congress Catalog Card Number: 78-157844.

International Standard Book Number:
0-87778-018-8.

Second Printing

FOREWORD

During the past decade a fascinating revolutionary movement has been evident in professional education. Changes in subject matter area structures and organization, staff utilization and school organization, instructional materials and techniques, as well as the philosophical and actual move toward individualization of instruction, have been so alarmingly rapid that the normal evolutionary pace has been disrupted. These revolutionary changes *per se* have caused an unusual amount of curriculum planning confusion and have complicated the decision making which must be done by elementary and secondary school personnel.

These revolutionary changes also brought to the forefront, as never before, the importance of systematic curriculum planning which leads to the improvement of instruction. And where such planning is on-going, teachers and other professional personnel in education need help, desperately. They need help at many points along the way; but, first and foremost, they need help in deciding what to teach and how to teach it.

In like manner, there is no longer any question about the need for individualized instruction for all students. The times demand it. The age in which we live is one which requires the maximum development of each individual's special talents. And this demand requires that students be given the opportunity to pursue their own unique objectives in their own unique ways. This is the mark of the times as opposed to teaching for identical objectives for all students in the same way. Again, this makes planning for instruction a tremendous task for even the very best of teachers. It multiplies the decisions about what to teach and how to teach by as many times as there are students in any school.

The following pages describe a program which began in 1963 and which was designed to help the teacher overcome this complicated planning task. The program employs the computer as a tool to aid the teacher in pre-planning units of instruction which contain a flexible array of teaching-learning situations for large groups, small groups, and individual students. Basically, in this program, the computer serves as a retrieval system which aids the teacher in his decision making about related topical objectives for groups of students, objectives for individual students, subject matter content, instructional activities, materials, and testing devices.

But the authors have described more than just a simple

retrieval program. They have presented for the reader a discussion of the entire area of using the computer as an aid for systematic teacher planning of curriculum and instruction. Supported by research studies, procedures, and practical guidelines, they have offered the teacher, as well as the curriculum worker, administrators, and others interested in the improvement of instruction a clear statement for getting started. The authors are obviously well qualified to do this, since they worked in public school situations writing, improving, developing, and managing the actual on-going computer-based resource unit program. Beyond that, they have been directly involved in educational research related to this overall area. Their involvement has demanded rigorous activity and careful thinking. They all speak from direct and personal experiences with the program. Therefore, this book will have great utility for the professional educator.

What is contained in these pages has been carried by word of mouth to thousands of interested persons. Many other requests for this information could not be adequately provided for because of the immensity of the task of passing along so much information. Within these covers are answers to many of the questions so often asked. Although new questions will arise, and new answers will be found, this book comprises a very useful contemporary exploration of the work in the area.

Robert S. Harnack
State University of New York
at Buffalo

PREFACE

For many years educators have been searching for ways of meeting the needs of individuals in their instructional programs. Schemes have come and gone, techniques have flourished and been forgotten, devices have been marketed and been rejected, and the obstacles to individualized instruction have prevailed. Teachers are busy and over-worked, teacher-pupil ratios are overwhelming, and some of the most obvious solutions demand more conformity than many teachers are willing to encourage. These are some of the challenges which face all educators today.

This is the era of technology, too. It is a time when technology can be harnessed to help educators overcome their problems. As a tool of this period, the electronic computer is unmatched in its potential to help teachers achieve truly individualized instruction. Furthermore, this remarkable device is not confined to presenting only highly structured linear programs for rote learning. The computer is capable of providing the kind of assistance necessary for teachers to diversify their objectives for instruction of individuals as well as their instructional procedures. This book is an attempt to describe such a program.

The attempt is made in the following pages to describe a process which can be employed to assist teachers in making decisions to plan a program of individualized instruction. This process is based upon a project which has been conducted in the Western New York area for the past several years. The original project was entitled "The Use of Electronic Computers to Improve Individualization of Instruction Through Unit Teaching," and was supported through a grant from the Cooperative Research Program (Project number D-112) of the Office of Education, U.S. Department of Health, Education, and Welfare under the direction of Robert S. Harnack. This project was the first of its kind to demonstrate that the computer could be used as a tool for curriculum planning and improvement. Three subsequent grants, two under the direction of the senior author and one directed by Thomas J. Clayback, funded under Title III of the Elementary-Secondary Education Act (Grant number: OEG-1-7-672947-2885), further demonstrated the feasibility of such an approach and added considerably to the data base which forms the substance of the retrieval system upon which the program is built. Meanwhile, numerous research studies have been completed which underscore the value of this approach in terms of learning outcomes and teacher behaviors. At present, several other projects are being conducted at various institutions which utilize the principles underlying the earlier work.

We feel that this work has resulted in some general concepts about using the computer to assist in the planning of curriculum and instruction. This book is devoted to an exploration of these concepts. Basically, we have attempted to develop a theoretical rationale, to give specific illustrations, to cite significant research, and to provide the prospective user with some suggestions for getting started. Specifically, the first chapter presents the theory behind using the computer to assist in the *planning* of curriculum and instruction; the second chapter describes one specific application of the theory; chapters three and four discuss the research findings which have implications for future developments; chapter five discusses the use of computer assisted planning as a means of conducting research and evaluation; chapter six provides a set of suggestions for the prospective user.

This work is intended to be a general treatment of computer assisted planning of curriculum and instruction. Obviously, many of the ideas are drawn from the experiences of the authors. However, insofar as possible, we have attempted to provide the kind of information which would enable others who are interested in the improvement and individualization of instruction to make use of a remarkable tool to facilitate the process—the computer.

The ideas upon which this work is based belong to many people, but principally they evolved from one man, Professor Robert S. Harnack, Chairman, Department of Curriculum Development and Instructional Media, State University of New York at Buffalo. To him we owe much. For whatever weakness exists, however, in the text of this work the authors accept full responsibility.

James E. Eisele

CONTENTS

Preface   *viii*

Chapter I: Computer   Assisted   Planning: A
               Rationale   *3*

                   An Instructional Model
                   Planning for Instruction
                   Planning Assistance
                   Computer Assisted Planning
                   Conclusion

Chapter II: Computer-Based   Resource   Guides
               for the Individualization of Instruc-
               tion   *20*

                   Objective
                   Procedures
                   Implementation
                   Feedback

Implications
Conclusion

Chapter III: Computer Assisted Planning for Specified Learning Outcomes   *49*

Resource Guides and Critical Thinking
Resource Guides and Attitudes Toward Mathematics
Resource Guides and Understanding
Resource Guides and Knowledge of Specifics
Conclusion

Chapter IV: Computer Assisted Planning and Instructional Behavior   *62*

Resource Guides and Preplanning
Changes in Instructional Behavior
Resource Guides and Team Teaching
Selection of Instructional Objectives
Conclusion

Chapter V: Computer Assisted Planning as a Vehicle for Curriculum Evaluation and Research   *74*

Vehicle for Research and
Evaluation
Research in Progress
Teacher and Teacher Training
Assessment
Conclusion

Chapter VI: Utilization and Implications of
Computer Assisted Planning of
Curriculum and Instruction   *85*

Utilization
Implications
Conclusion

Suggested Readings   *108*

Appendix A   *113*

Appendix B   *130*

COMPUTER ASSISTED PLANNING
OF
CURRICULUM AND INSTRUCTION

CHAPTER I

COMPUTER ASSISTED PLANNING: A RATIONALE

Much of the focus of instructional technology has been on the interaction between the student and a specific instructional sequence, or strategy. This is as it should be, for, in the final analysis, it is precisely this interaction which will result in the acquisition of modified behavior patterns on the part of the student.

Much of the glamour has also gone to innovations which focus on a direct tutorial relationship to students. Perhaps this is partly owing to the fact that anything which can be so utilized by individual students represents a tremendous potential market upon which business interests are anxious to capitalize.

An equally important concern which has received

considerably less attention, however, is the decision making which goes into the selection, by a school district, a school, or a classroom teacher, of specific instructional strategies. In other words, there should be as much emphasis placed upon the selection of a programmed text, for example, for a given child as there is on the development and marketing of the text. In short, there is a need for assistance with the planning of curricula for individuals.

Although the computer represents only one possible tool for the improvement of instruction, its data processing ability makes it particularly suitable for assistance in the planning of instruction. In essence, the computer provides a remarkable facility for storing data necessary for instructional planning and releasing portions of the data according to predetermined criteria. The process can be analogous to the teacher who can recall the titles of many textbooks and, upon request, can specify the ones most suitable for a certain task. Obviously, the capability of the computer to "remember" information is far greater than that of any individuals living today. When this capability is employed within the framework of decision making about all aspects of the curriculum, the process may be called *Computer Assisted Planning* for instruction, the topic of this book.

An Instructional Model
The nature of the instructional process may be an

elementary topic for most educators, but it is essential that any attempt to assist with the planning for instruction be based upon a comprehensive framework of the total process. Without this overall view there may be a tendency to overemphasize a single phase of the total process which appears more obvious than the others. For example, it is axiomatic that classroom teachers select textbooks for student use in their particular subject. To many people, this may appear to be the main planning function of the teacher. It becomes apparent that if this were viewed as *the* major planning function of the classroom teacher, one kind of retrieval system of specifying bibliographic data according to course titles would suffice. Unfortunately, this is merely one of the decisions teachers must make and, in fact, may not be made at all if the teacher is practicing individualized instruction. A more complete model of the process must include the components of needs assessment, goal selection, instructional procedure selection, and evaluation of progress. Each of these will be briefly discussed.

Needs Assessment

To some degree, all teachers make decisions about the needs of the learners in their classrooms. The level at which these needs are assessed by teachers may range from the simple analysis that all students *need* to learn mathematics (or history, grammar, etc.) to a thorough analysis of the background and interests of a particular student and a specific statement of his individual needs.

In many situations, choice-making about individual needs by the teacher or the student is considerably restricted by predetermined requirements. Even these, though, are based upon some concept about what the learner needs, whether couched in terms of human growth and development, society, philosophy, or the dictates of a logical structure of a discipline. In some cases, these requirements are translated into a prescribed set of experiences through which all students must pass with varying degrees of success.

In other instances, a careful analysis of data about an individual learner serves as a basis for planning an individualized curriculum. This may never be realized in most classrooms today, but the authors are firmly convinced that classroom teachers, in general, would like to approximate a curriculum based upon individual needs. Most teachers are quick to recognize that motivated and interested learners create the greatest rewards for the teacher, and that motivation is a function of their needs. However, it is equally true that the effort required to make judgments about the needs of individuals often exceeds the value of the results, especially given the present state of the art of needs assessment.

Goal Selection

Regardless of the level at which the needs of students are assumed, all teachers determine a point at which their efforts will be aimed, based upon the conception of student needs. Again, the level of specification can vary considerably, as with the ascertaining of needs. The determination of goals may range from a simple belief that the students will sit quietly for fifty minutes a day throughout a semester to a careful specification of individual behavioral objectives which cite a specific given situation, a proposed behavioral outcome, and a criterion for a level of performance indicative of the desirable outcome.

Once again, it is our conviction that teachers desire to set goals which are realistic in terms of the needs of learners and that they desire to phrase goals in behavioral terms. Certainly, not *all* teachers are striving to achieve the ultimate in this regard, but many already recognize the advantages of this approach and others are quick to agree when given the opportunity to experience the use of behavioral objectives and individualized instruction.

A major obstacle to widespread use of this approach is the overwhelming task of stating up to 750 behavioral objectives per week, if five classes of thirty students each were to work toward different objectives each day. This is obviously an exaggeration and a highly unlikely event, but is useful as a point of departure for estimating possible numbers of objectives required for individualized instruction.

Instructional Procedures
The intervention strategies employed by the teacher to

enable the student to modify his behavior from point A to point B can be called instructional procedures. In theory, at least, all instructional procedures serve as the vehicle for the attainment of the objectives, although in practice their utility and relevance are often questioned. Nevertheless, most teachers believe that the procedures they employ will contribute to the desired ends, and hardly ever would a teacher *purposely* use procedures that would prevent the achievement of the objectives.

Instructional procedures can be thought of as messages[1] to be received by the student. They have content (the subject matter used); elements and structure (instructional activities organized into some sequence with definable scope); and a code and treatment (medium and form used for transmission).

The design of instructional procedures for the attainment of specified goals is not widely practiced by educators. Typical expectations often preclude such choice-making as is necessary for purposeful design of instructional procedures. Sometimes the best that can be accomplished in this regard is to select the lesser of the evils among the *given* alternatives. Such might be the case in selecting textbooks from among the meagre supply available in most classrooms. Ideally, the selection or design of procedures should be made without such constraints and should represent the best hypothetical approach which can be conceived and eventually tested.

Evaluation

Evaluation is the process whereby judgments are made about the progress of the student in attaining the objectives. The fundamental purpose is to provide information about this progress which will permit alterations in the procedures to ensure eventual attainment of the objectives. If progress is satisfactory in terms of overall expectations, then changes in instructional procedures may be minimal or not required at all. If progress is less than is expected or desired, drastic changes may be required in any part or all of the procedures previously employed.

Secondarily, evaluation serves as a forerunner of needs assessment. Evaluation is made in terms of objectives, however, not needs. Once it is established that certain objectives have been achieved, these data about the learner are useful for identifying subsequent needs which may include those already identified.

Planning for Instruction

Obviously, the key to effective instruction is decision making. Decisions made about any element of the above described model can determine the quality of the total process. In this sense, the choice of a single teaching machine over other media is as important as the selection of objectives or assessment of needs. The ideal state might be for all decisions to be made in light of valid and reliable research evidence by informed experts in all of the areas described in the model. However, to even approach this ideal, there is a necessary precondition: planning.

As indicated, choices made by humans may not always be perfect, because they are subject to human error and fallibility. It must also be recognized that some decision making is of a better quality than is some other. Simply, if the use of a film results in the attainment of an objective when the use of a series of slides was not as successful, all other things being equal, then the decision to use the film was "better" than the decision to use the slide series. But how does the teacher know enough to make the decision to use the film over the slide? The answer is "planning."

Only through planning can the improvement of teacher decision making be assured. Experimentation is an essential aspect of planning, but experimentation alone is not sufficient. It is during the process of planning that experimental data can be considered in making choices about instruction. Without this consideration, many valuable research results may be doomed to " rest in peace" in the annals of research conferences or in the yellowing pages of journals. The greatest fruits of research will only be realized when research results are used in evidence to make appropriate educational choices.

Briefly, the planning which is necessary in view of the above-described instructional model is as follows. What kind of data are necessary to determine individual needs, how can they be obtained, and how are they to be handled? Which instructional objectives are relevant to what kinds of learner needs, and how can these objectives be derived? Which instructional procedures are best for achieving given objectives and for specific individuals with their own unique characteristics and learning styles, and how can these be determined, organized, and implemented? Which evaluation procedures and devices are best for given objectives and for specific individuals, and how can these be determined and/or acquired and utilized? In general, what is the best way to go about answering these questions?

Granted, finding answers to these questions is a tall order. Furthermore, these may be merely the most obvious questions which need to be answered. Certainly, each question assumes that many others will be answered in the process of planning. There may be many left out of the above listing. But, essentially, providing the answers to those questions posed will constitute a giant step in the planning of an individualized curriculum.

Planning Assistance

Planning for instruction has been a topic of major concern for many years. The excellent books written on the subject are too numerous to begin to recite in this space. Names such as Alberty, Alexander, Caswell, Crosby, Doll, Herrick, Krug, Saylor, Shores, Smith, Stanley, Taba, and

Tyler, to mention only a few, are major proponents of effective curriculum planning. The famous Eight-Year Study made substantial contributions to increasing the effectiveness of the planning process. Many gains have been made as a result of the research and writing of these persons and those associated with the Eight-Year Study. Almost unanimously, answers to the previously cited questions were sought, as well as were ways of seeking the answers.

One result of the efforts of many leading scholars is the use of the unit approach to preplanning teaching-learning situations. Of the many definitions of this approach available in the literature, Gwynn and Chase offer this concise statement:

> . . . the unit method . . . has been an attempt to integrate and arrange the curriculum so that the child could achieve mastery of the desired objectives in education in a meaningful and permanent manner.[2]

In a sense, then, any attempt to organize teaching plans so that learning is purposeful can be construed as unit teaching. One further concept, however, is integral to the unit approach. This is alluded to by Gwynn when he talks about integrating and arranging the curriculum so that learning is meaningful and permanent. Oliver speaks more directly to the point:

> Of course, the real advantage of the unit plan lies in the extent to which the principle of unity is realized. This unification, or *integration,* takes place in two realms—in the content and within the learner. The world is full of content (knowledge);

the function of education is to so order it that relationships are brought out. Isolated facts and scattered skills are difficult to comprehend and hence to remember; if they can be organized to show their "relatedness," they can be "learned" better. In selecting knowledges that will have a bearing on some unifying element, the curriculum worker will be effecting the integration of content. This, however, is external to the pupil, since *his* learning comes when the relationships are established within him. It is assumed, therefore, that organizing classroom activities into units will facilitate individual, internal integration. In short, the unit approach is psychologically sound. If the point of unity is of significance to the learner, then learning will be further promoted, since psychologists believe that individuals are motivated to learn in (1) a problem situation and (2) in a setting that is real and meaningful.[3]

In addition to possessing the characteristics of purpose and unity, unit plans usually include some combinations of suggestions for instructional objectives, content, activities, materials, and evaluation devices and/or procedures. The assistance which these plans offer for planning for instruction comes by way of increasing the alternatives from which the final selection can be made, thus increasing the likelihood of choosing the best instructional procedures, within the framework of a unifying theme.

The concept of unit teaching is as popular today as ever. A review of the major projects which constitute the so-called curriculum revolution of the past decade reveals similarities between these and the unit approach. To mention only a few, the following "innovations" all contain in some form the elements of which units consist: Biological Sciences Curriculum Study, Physical Sciences Study Commission Curriculum, Science: A Process Approach, Individually Prescribed Instruction, Project on Learning in Accordance with Needs, and The Contract Method, as well as most schemes for individualizing instruction.

The unit approach, including the more recent adaptations described above, has not been without its shortcomings. The demand for considerable time to make decisions about which objectives, procedures and evaluation devices to use with individuals has presented an insurmountable obstacle to the intelligent use of this approach. The demand for knowledge about the use of many different instructional procedures, and for the availability of materials and facilities for using them, has been another almost insurmountable barrier. Also, among the most apparent problems, the lack of an effective means of revising all unit plans has resulted in rapid obsolescence of even the best of those devised. Furthermore, the inability to easily and efficiently revise units has meant that some well-intentioned plans were never widely utilized because, without revision, their shortcomings were simply too extensive. Perhaps the greatest of all obstacles to widespread adoption of this purposeful approach to teaching has been the lack of effective means of disseminating well-planned units. Until recently, when national groups and private publishers began mass production of specific plans, many excellent units never left the area where they were developed, and were soon forgotten.

Computer Assisted Planning

What has been discussed so far is the kind of assistance which has been available in the past to help teachers make decisions and to plan a curriculum for individuals. Further, several shortcomings of most of these attempts have been pointed out. It is now time to indicate that the computer, while not a panacea, possesses capabilities which drastically reduce many of the aforementioned problems and can, potentially, provide teachers with remarkable assistance for planning, organizing, and implementing an individualized curriculum.

A review of teacher decision making functions will be useful here. Concisely stated, a teacher must:

1. Decide upon learning outcomes which are appropriate for the class and individuals in the class.

2. Decide upon the content or subject matter which is related to the desirable learning outcomes.

3. Decide upon instructional activities which will introduce the behavior to be learned to the student, will provide opportunities for acquiring the behavior, and will give the learner opportunities to practice the behavior.

4. Decide upon media which will transmit the data

which is to be learned.

5. Decide upon evaluation procedures and devices.

6. Decide which of the above selected content (function #2) is appropriate for each individual in the class.

7. Decide which of the above (function #3) determined activities are appropriate for each learner.

8. Decide which of the above (function #4) media are appropriate for each learner.

9. Decide which of the above (function #5) evaluation procedures and devices are appropriate for each learner.

Furthermore, the above decisions should be made within the context of an integrated, meaningful framework if this is, in fact, the way in which people learn best.

What should be emerging at this point is the notion that many of the above functions or decisions are really a process of matching items to certain criteria, e.g., which books match which objectives and, of these, which ones match a given reading level of a specific student. Or, in other words, *many decisions are really data processing functions* which may be done best by automatic data processing equipment, i.e., a computer.

The advantages of using a computer to facilitate the above described decision making can be numerous. First, the computer can store much more data than can the human mind and can make the retrieval of the data quickly and efficiently. Second, the computer can process the data much more quickly than can the human mind, and with far greater ease. For example, list all the books which are useful for gaining skill at making generalizations about social, political, economic, and religious conditions which precede international warfare. Next, separate all those books listed into different reading levels, then into interest categories. This task is monumental for a human, especially when multiplied by numerous objectives, many more categories than reading level and interest areas, and different kinds of media. For the human mind, even extensive preparation cannot combat the effects of forgetting and preoccupation. For the computer, the task is reduced to appropriate programming.

Another advantage of the computer is the capability of communicating data over long distances in short periods of time. Perhaps most significant, however, is the regenerative capability of the computer. Data can be altered in many ways through relatively simple procedures. Errors can be easily corrected, new data can be conveniently added, and obsolete data can be quickly removed. This facility provides for updating which cannot be matched by any other means at the present time. It is hoped that these, and other advantages, will become apparent in the more thorough discussion of a specific application of Computer Assisted Planning of Instruction which follows in the next chapters.

Conclusion

It is possible to distinguish many decision making

functions of a classroom teacher in planning for individualized instruction. This is possible through an analysis of the kinds of decisions teachers make relative to a descriptive model of the elements of the instructional process—in short, determining appropriate objectives based upon individual needs, selecting instructional procedures for attaining the objectives, and deciding upon a means of evaluating progress.

Many of the choices for individualizing instruction require routine decision making functions. Functions such as matching specific media with certain objectives can become routinized. That is, if a given medium is appropriate for a given objective, its selection will become routine, until there is a change in its appropriateness, of course. These routine functions are ideally suited to the capabilities of the computer. Once directed to perform the routine decision making task, the computer will obey consistently and continuously until given a change in directions.

Where other attempts to provide assistance in planning an appropriate individualized curriculum have failed, the use of the computer may admirably succeed. Its capability for storage, processing, and retrieval of data exceeds anything that has been previously known to man. In the following chapter a unique application of this remarkable tool for the planning of instruction will be described.

References

1.   See Berlo's Model in David K. Berlo. *The Process of*

Communication. New York: Holt, Rinehart and Winston, Inc., 1960, 72.

2. J. Minor Gwynn and John B. Chase, Jr. *Curriculum Principles and Social Trends.* New York: The Macmillan Company, 1969, 179.

3. Albert I. Oliver. *Curriculum Improvement.* New York: Dodd, Mead and Company, 1965, 348.

CHAPTER II

COMPUTER-BASED RESOURCE GUIDES FOR THE INDIVIDUALIZATION OF INSTRUCTION

Computer-Based Resource Guides are one attempt to use the computer to assist teachers to preplan an individualized program of instruction for students. The instructional rationale for this project has been described in the preceding chapter. In this chapter an attempt will be made to describe, in some detail, the actual workings of this approach.

Initially, the field was searched for answers to the following questions:

1. What processes are employed by the expert classroom teacher in making decisions about individual teaching-learning situations?

2. What variables must be considered in making de-

cisions about teaching and learning plans?

3. Can the computer be used to augment the decision making powers of the classroom teacher?

The job of the teacher seems clear in some respects. He is expected to provide learning opportunities for each student which are in keeping with the needs of the individual. He must select these opportunities either from his own experiences or from these experiences in combination with other data sources. And the individual programs must account for a host of variables which at present are hypothesized to be related to the learning process. Examples of these variables would be learning rate, learning styles, interests, cognitive stages, and sex.

Another expectation of the teacher is that the individualized curriculum is significant in terms of the discipline and is organized for optimum learning conditions. This adds considerably to the complexity of the decision making function of the teacher. In all, the operations necessary to satisfy the requirements mentioned, and countless more could no doubt be added, are sufficient to stagger the imagination. To get a rough quantitative estimate of the proportions of the task, consider only the number of behavioral objectives which would need to be written for an individualized program. Eisner[1] has estimated as many as 4,200 per year. This has been questioned as a bit high, but Sullivan's[2] estimate of 9-12 objectives for six or seven classes per day is still immense.

Objective

The major objective was to discover an effective means by which teachers could have available sufficient data to make decisions in preplanning individual teaching-learning situations. More specifically, an attempt was made to determine the kinds of decisions teachers must make to preplan an individual teaching-learning situation, what variables must be considered in the process, and what should be the outcome of the resulting decision making. Next, an attempt was made to conceptualize the teaching-learning process in order to provide a framework upon which a model could be developed. Finally, the intention was to apply automated procedures to the system, either in whole or in part.

Necessary criteria for any prospective system were that it had to 1) support the functions of the classroom teacher, 2) save him time, and 3) assist him with the more routine decision making functions. In addition, it was felt that the system should ultimately allow teachers to improve the quality of their decisions to permit more effective learning.

Procedures

The initial procedure in the development of the computer retrieval system was, of course, to specify the exact desired objectives for the system. To do this, it was necessary to differentiate between the desired functions of the teacher and those of the computer in terms of decisions which must be made in order to preplan a series of teaching-learning situations. The following breakdown has been reported by Harnack[3].

The teacher's functions were four in number:

1. To identify the subject of the teaching unit and the basic unifying theme which would serve as the center of interest in the classroom during a specific period of time.

2. To define the student's abilities, needs, characteristics, and interests, as these items relate to the selections to be made within the total unit.

3. To suggest possible learning outcomes in the form of behavioral skills, understandings, information, and peripheral objectives which may reasonably be expected to result from the teaching-learning situations developed throughout the unit.

4. To make, if deemed necessary, certain professional decisions related to those tasks or areas which the teacher deems important for the objectives and the students in the classroom.

On the other hand, the electronic computer had to satisfy the following functions:

1. To provide the teacher with a subject matter outline or problem census related to the learning outcomes identified by the teacher.

2. To suggest a significant (related to the learning outcomes and characteristics of the pupils) number of large-group introductory, developmental, and culminating activities.

3. To suggest a significant number of introductory,

developmental, and culminating small-group activities.
4. To suggest a significant number of individual learning activities which might prove to be helpful.
5. To suggest suitable instructional materials, including reference materials, for individual students.
6. To suggest appropriate equipment, audiovisual materials, and the like, for large-group and small-group instruction.
7. To suggest suitable references and other materials for the use of the teacher.
8. To suggest how achievement of these proposed outcomes may be evaluated.
9. To suggest "leads" to other related units (continuous activities) which might grow out of the proposed unit.

The teaching model around which the program was built can be roughly summarized here. According to this model, the teacher first determines an area of interest around which several related teaching-learning situations can be developed. He then selects or identifies the specific behavioral objectives related to the topic, which the learners can reasonably be expected to achieve *based upon their needs.* From some reservoir of ideas, then, the teacher selects items related to objectives held in common to all for large-group instruction. These items include the subject matter, materials, procedures, and evaluative criteria—the screen for selection of these items in this case being the selected objective. There seems to be no reason why, if the criterion for selection (the objective) is known, the related items could not be stored and retrieved whenever the objective is called for.

The next step in the model is to identify the characteristics of individual learners which should serve as screens in selecting items related to an objective for a specific learner. Given an objective, for example, for which several instructional items are appropriate, the teacher will select those which are most suitable for a specific individual. To cite a common illustration of this kind of screen, of several books related to a given objective the teacher would select the ones which the learner could read, or which match an individual's reading level.

Programs were written which employed the objectives and variables called learner characteristics as screens. A complete listing of these variables can be found in Illustration I. A third screen was also developed to permit teachers to exercise their judgment in selecting items which were in keeping with factors relevant to special knowledge about teaching, such as methods of instruction, types of objectives, and types or kinds of instructional materials. These were called professional decision making variables and are listed in Illustration II.

To operationalize the system, items were written for each component within the framework of units which were commonly taught in elementary school or high school. Behavioral objectives, subject matter broken into short statements or in outline form, suggested instructional procedures, materials and references, and evaluation procedures were written. Each item was assigned an identifying numeral and symbol. For example, OB 17 refers to objective number 17, and SM 34 refers to the item of subject matter numbered

34. Each item of subject matter, instructional activity, material, and evaluation devices is then "coded" by specifying the numerals of the objectives to which each relates. For example, MA 13-2,7,44 means that material number 13 is appropriate for objectives numbered 2, 7, and 44 in the unit. Topics are also assigned identifying numerals.

(continued on Page 33)

Illustration I

LEARNER VARIABLES

General Interests

1 Philosophy	2 Psychology
3 Logic	4 Morals
5 Religion	6 Political Science
7 Economics	8 Law
9 Education	10 Commerce
11 Everyday Experiences	12 Folklore
13 Language	14 Astronomy
15 Chemistry	16 Earth Science
17 Mathematics	18 Physics
19 Anthropology	20 Biological Science
21 Engineering	22 Agriculture
23 Domestic Science	24 Other Places
25 Animals	26 Famous People
27 Natural Phenomenon	28 Creating and Construction
29 Fine Arts	30 Photography
31 Biography or Autobiography	32 Drama
33 Fiction	34 Poetry

Illustration I (continued)

35 Geography	36 History
37 Sports/Leisure	38 Social Science
39 Physical Science	40 Natural Science
41 Humanities	42 Music
43 Art	44 Creative Writing
45 Adventure	46 Non-Fiction
47 Early Days	48 Modern Wonders
49 Old Tales	50 Fun
51 Automobiles	52 Transportation

Occupational Interests

53 Industry	54 Communications
55 Transportation	56 Homemaking/Home Nursing/Child Care
57 Food/Agriculture	58 Finance
59 Business/Office	60 Sales/Marketing
61 Recreation/Travel	62 Service
63 Construction	64 Arts and Entertainment
65 Science/Research	

Social Class

66 Lower/Lower	67 Upper/Lower
68 Lower/Middle	69 Upper/Middle
70 Lower/Upper	71 Upper/Upper

Sex

72 Male	73 Female

Developmental Tasks

74 Learning Physical Skills Necessary for Ordinary Games
75 Building Wholesome Attitudes Toward Oneself as a Growing Organism

Illustration I (continued)

76 Learning to Get Along with Age-Mates
77 Learning an Appropriate Masculine or Feminine Social Role
78 Developing Fundamental Skills in Reading, Writing and Calculating
79 Developing Concepts Necessary for Everyday Living
80 Developing Conscience, Morality, and a System of Values
81 Achieving Personal Independence
82 Developing Attitudes Toward Social Groups and Institutions
83 Accepting New and More Mature Relations with Age-Mates of Both Sexes
84 Accepting One's Physique (Male and Female Role)
85 Achieving Emotional Independence from Parents and Other Adults
86 Achieving Assurances of Economic Independence
87 Selecting and Preparing for an Occupation
88 Developing Intellectual Skills and Concepts Necessary for Civic Competence
89 Desiring and Achieving Socially Responsible Behavior
90 Preparing for Marriage and Family Life
91 Acquiring a Set of Values and Ethical System as a Guide to Behavior

Reading Level

103	Non-Reader	104	Pre-Primer
105	Primer	106	1
107	1.5	108	2
109	2.5	110	3
111	4	112	5
113	6	114	7

Illustration I (continued)

115	8	116	9
117	10	118	11
119	12	120	Above 12

Mental Age

194	.5	195	1.0
196	1.5	197	2.0
198	2.5	199	3.0
200	3.5	201	4.0
202	5.0	203	6.0
204	7.0	205	8.0
206	9.0	207	10.0
208	11.0	209	12.0
210	13.0	211	14.0
212	15.0	213	16.0
214	17.0	215	18.0
216	19.0	217	20.0
218	Above 20		

Chronological Age

219	0.5	220	1.0
221	1.5	222	2.0
223	2.5	224	3.0
225	4.0	226	5.0
227	6.0	228	7.0
229	8.0	230	9.0
231	10.0	232	11.0
233	12.0	234	13.0
235	14.0	236	15.0
237	16.0	238	17.0
239	18.0	240	19.0
241	20.0	242	21.0

Illustration I (continued)

Physical Handicaps

243 Blind

244 Partially Sighted

245 Deaf

246 Hard of Hearing

247 Gross Motor Disability

248 Fine Motor Disability

Residential Status

252 Residential

253 Non-Residential

Body Area

254 Head, Neck, Shoulders

255 Arms

256 Trunk, Lungs

257 Legs, Feet

Learning Environment

258 Classroom

259 Outdoors

260 Gymnasium

Illustration II

PROFESSIONAL DECISION MAKING VARIABLES

Major Social Function

92 Governing	93 Communicating
94 Transporting	95 Producing
96 Consuming and Conserving	97 Heritage
98 Cooperating	99 Leisure
100 Earning a Living	101 Educating
102 Spiritual/Moral	

Instructional Activity

121 Teacher Activity	122 Dramatization
123 Verbal	124 Non-Verbal
125 Problem Solving	126 Reading
127 Field Trips	128 Writing
129 Listening	130 Speaking
131 Constructing/Creating	132 Laboratory
133 Drill/Practice	134 Physical/Tactile
135 Lecture	136 Teacher Led Discussion
137 Student Led Discussion	138 Recitation

Suggested Approach

139 Introductory Activity	140 Developmental Activity
141 Culminating Activity	142 Extra-Curricular Activity

Objectives

143 Knowledge	144 Comprehension
145 Application	146 Analysis
147 Synthesis	148 Evaluation
149 Receiving	150 Responding
151 Valuing	152 Organization

Illustration II (continued)

153 Characterization by a   154 Psychomotor
    Value

Material Descriptor
155 Audio   156 Visual
157 Audiovisual   158 Verbal
159 Non-Verbal   160 Printed
161 Programmed Instruction   162 3-D Material/Laboratory
163 Resource/Places/People

Materials
164 Books   165 Vertical File Material
166 Films   167 Filmstrips
168 Resource People   169 Resource Places
170 Charts   171 Maps
172 Blackboard Design   173 Bulletin Board
                                  Design Materials

174 Opaque Projector   175 Overhead Projector
    Materials
176 Sponsored Materials   177 Programmed Materials
178 Tapes   179 Records
180 Slides   181 Art Materials

Instructional Grouping
182 Student Activities   183 Small-Group Activity
    (individual)
184 Large-Group Activity

Evaluation Devices
185 Standardized Test   186 Paper/Pencil Essay
187 Paper/Pencil Objective   188 Rating Scale
189 Checklist   190 Log/Diary

Illustration II (continued)

191 Self-Evaluation   192 Creating and/or
                                  Construction
193 Selective Observation

Each item, including objectives, is then coded to the learner and professional variables by indicating the variable number to which the item relates. At present there are a total of 260 variables to which an item could be related.

Implementation

To use the system which has just been described, the potential user initially requests a listing of the objectives for any of the available units. A sample set of these objectives appears in Appendix A. Note, particularly, that they are listed according to the categories of the *Taxonomy of Educational Objectives,*[4] although not numbered chronologically according to these categories (numbers in parenthesis refer to the order in which they were originally presented for coding). A listing of the units presently available can be found in Appendix B.

From the listing of objectives which the teacher subsequently receives, a selection is made of those desired for the total class of students, and those desired for each individual in the class. These selections are indicated on forms which accompany the listing of objectives. Also on a form provided (Illustration III), the teacher completes a profile for each learner indicating the characteristics which best apply to each one.

After returning the request materials to the point of origination, the computer can generate any of the four sets of suggestions labeled Parts A, B, C, and D in Illustration IV. The choice of which combination of suggestions is desired is optional for the user. Part A lists all content, activities, materials, and measuring devices for each objective chosen. Part B does the same for each individual, listing only those items which match the individual's characteristics. Part C provides only a listing of instructional materials and measuring devices which are necessary for implementing the unit.

(continued on Page 40)

Illustration III

PUPIL PROFILE

Instructions: Write the *code numbers* of the variables which apply to each student on the Request Form.

General Interests

01 Philosophy	27 Natural Phenomenon
02 Psychology	28 Creating and Construction
03 Logic	29 Fine Arts
04 Morals	30 Photography

Illustration III (continued)

05 Religion	31 Biography or Autobiography
06 Political Science	32 Drama
07 Economics	33 Fiction
08 Law	34 Poetry
09 Education	35 Geography
10 Commerce	36 History
11 Everyday Experiences	37 Sports/Leisure
12 Folklore	38 Social Science
13 Language	39 Physical Science
14 Astronomy	40 Natural Science
15 Chemistry	41 Humanities
16 Earth Science	42 Music
17 Mathematics	43 Art
18 Physics	44 Creative Writing
19 Anthropology	45 Adventure
20 Biological Science	46 Non-Fiction
21 Engineering	47 Early Days
22 Agriculture	48 Modern Wonders
23 Home Economics	49 Old Tales
24 Other Places	50 Fun
25 Animals	51 Automobiles
26 Famous People	52 Transportation

Occupational Interests (Optional)

53 Industry	59 Business/Office
54 Communication	60 Sales/Marketing
55 Transportation	61 Recreation/Travel
56 Homemaking/Home Nursing/Child Care	62 Service
	63 Construction
57 Food/Agriculture	64 Arts and Entertainment
58 Finance	65 Science/Research

Illustration III (continued)

Developmental Tasks (Optional)

74 Learning Physical Skills Necessary for Ordinary Games
75 Building Wholesome Attitudes Toward Oneself as a Growing Organism
76 Learning to Get Along with Age-Mates
77 Learning an Appropriate Masculine or Feminine Social Role
78 Developing Fundamental Skills in Reading, Writing, and Calculating
79 Developing Concepts Necessary for Everyday Living
80 Developing Conscience, Morality, and a System of Values
81 Achieving Personal Independence
82 Developing Attitudes Toward Social Groups and Institutions
83 Accepting New and More Mature Relations with Age-Mates of Both Sexes
84 Accepting One's Physique (Male and Female Role)
85 Achieving Emotional Independence from Parents and Other Adults
86 Achieving Assurances of Economic Independence
87 Selecting and Preparing for an Occupation
88 Developing Intellectual Skills and Concepts Necessary for Civic Competence
89 Desiring and Achieving Socially Responsible Behavior
90 Preparing for Marriage and Family Life
91 Acquiring a Set of Values and Ethical System as a Guide to Behavior

Illustration III (continued)

Reading Level (Relative to Grade Level)

103	Non-Reader	112	5
104	Pre-Primer	113	6
105	Primer	114	7
106	1	115	8
107	1.5	116	9
108	2	117	10
109	2.5	118	11
110	3	119	12
111	4	120	Above 12

Mental Age

194	.5	206	10.0
195	1.0	207	11.0
196	1.5	208	12.0
197	2.0	209	13.0
198	2.5	210	14.0
199	3.0	211	15.0
200	4.0	212	16.0
201	5.0	213	17.0
202	6.0	214	18.0
203	7.0	215	19.0
204	8.0	216	20.0
205	9.0	217	Above 20

Chronological Age

218	0.5	230	10.0
219	1.0	231	11.0
220	1.5	232	12.0
221	2.0	233	13.0
222	2.5	234	14.0
223	3.0	235	15.0

Illustration III (continued)

224	4.0	236	16.0
225	5.0	237	17.0
226	6.0	238	18.0
227	7.0	239	19.0
228	8.0	240	20.0
229	9.0	241	21.0

Illustration IV

Diagram of CBRU Schema

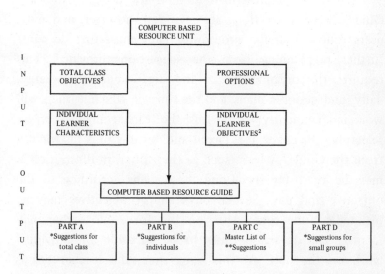

A Computer-Based Resource Unit consists of thousands of suggestions* for instructional strategies. Each of these suggestions is "coded" to the objectives in that particular unit as well as appropriate learner characteristics and professional variables. This coding acts as a screening device so that a classroom teacher will receive only those suggestions relevant to her particular students and situation.

* Suggestions include:	Objectives, content outline, activities, instructional materials, and measuring devices.
** Suggestions:	Part C contains only materials and measuring devices.

Part D provides a listing of suggestions for small groups of students who share a common objective.

There is no prescribed method for using a Resource Guide. Some suggestions are provided, however, and most users follow a similar procedure. They must first do some further preplanning from the suggestions provided. This requires the organization of the suggestions into weekly, daily, and periodic plans, and the times in which learners will work independently. To do this, the teacher might begin by selecting objectives for large- and small-group instruction from the Guide. A form such as that found in Illustration V may be used for specifying these plans according to the objective and day. Several days and/or objectives may be planned at one time. Also, on this form the teacher may identify the days and times to be set aside for individual work on the unit. At this same time, the teacher begins preplanning the individual work. Another form (Illustration VI) may be used to indicate the activities and materials for as many objectives as the teacher wishes to specify in advance. In some cases, preplanning for an individual pupil may involve a single objective at a time. In other cases, the student may experience longer range planning and may be expected to organize his time for more extensive periods. This form may be attached to the individual print-out and used for record-keeping purposes.

As soon as face-to-face interaction between teacher and pupils begins, it is desirable to involve the learner in as much planning as possible. Of course, they may have already been involved in the selection of objectives and other preliminary planning. At this point, they can profitably be involved in finalizing their individual and group plans with frequent opportunities for revision as they proceed through the unit.

In addition, it is necessary to make a concerted effort to provide the materials and measuring devices which are specified in the print-outs. This provision greatly increases the utility of the units and is the justification for providing Part C of the unit (Illustration IV). Just who assumes responsibility for this provision is not always clear, but the existence of library and media utilization personnel is highly desirable.

Feedback

The system is refined through a continuous source of feedback. The data bank is stored on magnetic tape while a matching tape collects feedback information about the items in a unit. Periodically, according to volume of use, the feedback tape provides data which indicate appropriate alterations to the unit. Changes are made in the master tape to either add to, delete, or alter items as confirming data is received from various sources which will be referred to later.

It must be remembered that the total system is based upon considered, and not experimentally tested, hypotheses. They are now, however, in testable form as further indicated

Illustration V

PLANNING GUIDE

Objective No. .... Day ....
(Briefly describe activity below)

Objective No. .... Day ....
(Briefly describe activity below)

Objective No. .... Day ....
(Briefly describe activity below)

Objective No. .... Day ....
(Briefly describe activity below)

Illustration VI

INDIVIDUAL PLANNING GUIDE

Name ....

Objective No. ....

Individual Activities	Check when completed
....	....
....	....
....	....
....	....
....	....
....	....
....	....
....	....
....	....
....	....
....	....
....	....

in Chapter V. Rather than disregarding untested procedures, this system provides a framework for their examination. The result of the experimentation is one valuable source of feedback; classroom teachers who use the system are another and are systematically solicited under current monitoring procedures.

Implications

The possibilities of this system seem unlimited. Some of the more salient ones are the saving of valuable teacher time, the availability of an extensive resource file in the data bank, a viable research framework, and the ability to individualize instruction.

With reference to the time factor, this system can save countless hours of preplanning time. The system makes many decisions of selection and matching which the teacher no longer has to make. These are routine decisions and should not be considered an abrogation of the teacher's rights or responsibilities. The result of this process frees the teacher to work more extensively with individual learners and to make decisions related to individual needs, progress, etc.

Of equal importance is the tremendous value of the data bank. Altogether, there now exist over five thousand objectives which are "taxonomized" and coded to a large number of other variables. In addition, there are countless items of subject matter, instructional procedures, materials, and evaluation devices also coded to the variables and related to the behavioral objectives. Furthermore, these are all related to instructional topics, the importance of which many of us have forgotten. The significance of the data bank to teaching and learning was documented in the preceding chapter in the discussion of the unit approach.

Another implication must deal with the timely topic of instruction. To vary instructional plans for a single objective requires tremendous knowledge and resources which most teachers simply do not have available. To also vary the objectives for individual students is almost more than anyone should expect of a teacher. This system can help by providing much of the necessary data for planning such an individualized program. Another project (discussed in Chapter VI) is preparing a pupil data file which will keep records on both learner characteristics and achievement. This file can be useful to both assist in the selection of objectives and as a screen for selecting individual programs of instruction.

Finally, the research framework of the system should be mentioned here, again. All combinations of a Resource Guide must be viewed as researchable hypotheses. Does treatment X result in condition Y and, if so, under what conditions? Do sex, age, etc., have any bearing on instructional decisions for specific objectives? The whole question of sequence and scope are researchable within this framework. Chapter V deals with this topic, but its significance bears this repetition.

Conclusion

The system which has been described has been used successfully to assist classroom teachers in individualizing instruction. It has demonstrated that some, although certainly not all, of the decision making processes of the classroom teacher can be augmented with electronic data processing equipment. Further, such augmentation enables the teacher to consider many variables when preplanning individual programs which could not be considered without such assistance. Research results which bear out these conclusions are reported in the next two chapters.

Many questions remain to be answered. Ultimately, the system must be judged in terms of learning outcomes, and data along these lines are constantly being gathered. Also, however, its effectiveness must be judged in terms of making curriculum and instruction more functional, assuming equal achievement on the part of the learners. Evidence of this nature is also being collected, and the results are most encouraging that this kind of assistance is being provided by the system. The nature of the teaching-learning process and the kinds of processes necessary to preplan units of instruction must continue to be investigated. An especially challenging and interesting area of research in connection with the system is the relevance of learners' characteristics to teaching and learning. Research is only beginning to touch upon these variables.

In conclusion, while recognizing many of the limitations

of the system and while better approaches are continually sought, this system seems to contribute much to a concern which has been described by Goodlad:

> If individualizing instruction is to become more than a slogan, data to guide diagnosis, information on the consequences of decisions, and data to facilitate reassessment are essential. The quantities and varieties of data to be stored and retrieved, to say nothing of the manipulations of these data to be performed, defy human capabilities. We are now beginning to envision for the teacher a highly professional role of diagnosing and prescribing for the learner. But this role may never be fulfilled unless the computer is brought meaningfully and productively into these sensitive, often intuitive, acts, as supplier of essential data and as predictor of certain possible consequences of choice. As yet this fertile soil has been scarcely gazed upon.[5]

References

1. W. James Popham, *et al. Instructional Objectives.* Chicago: Rand-McNally and Company, 1969, p. 14.
2. *Ibid.,* p. 55.
3. Robert S. Harnack. "Resource Units and the Computer." *The High School Journal,* December, 1967, pp. 127-128.
4. Benjamin S. Bloom (ed.), *et al. Taxonomy of Educational Objectives, Handbook I: Cognitive Domain.* 1956, and David R. Krathwohl, Benjamin S. Bloom, and Bertram B. Masia. *Taxonomy of Educational Objectives, Handbook II: Affective Domain.* New York: David

McKay Company, Inc., 1964.

5.   John I. Goodlad, *et al. Application of Electronic Data Processing Methods in Education.* Cooperative Research Program, U.S. Office of Education, Project No. F-026, University of California, Los Angeles, California, January, 1965.

CHAPTER III

COMPUTER ASSISTED PLANNING FOR SPECIFIED LEARNING OUTCOMES*

In the final analysis, the value of any curriculum or instructional innovation must be judged by its effects on student learning. Changes in behavior—cognitive, affective, and psychomotor—are the products of any curriculum and instructional program. There is, of course, also the need to make judgments about the processes associated with curriculum and instructional changes. Both kinds of evaluation are important in studying any proposed changes.

This chapter focuses on studies which examine the results on learning of using computer assisted planning. As

* This chapter was written by **Kenneth A. Cross**.

with much educational research, many of the findings reported herein did not attain acceptable levels of statistical significance. However, this factor is carefully considered when drawing inferences about the value of Computer Assisted Planning, as are those results which were statistically significant. Since the statistical analyses employed were two-tailed tests (i.e., testing for differences for the better or the worse), the non-significant results led the investigators to conclude that, in many cases, there were no differences in performance between groups utilizing Computer Assisted Planning and those using other approaches. On the other hand, what significant differences were found favored the experimental groups, in the main.

These factors, as well as some others which must be considered are, generally speaking, sufficient cause for encouragement. That is to say, there are three general statements about the studies conducted thus far which undergird future development of the procedures described in earlier chapters. These statements can be summarized as follows:

1. In almost all comparisons of computer assisted planning with other methods, gains in learning are either not unequal or are significantly greater for the experimental groups in relation to the control groups. In other words, as a result of using computer assisted planning, there are no quantitative losses and there are some quantitative gains.

2. As the next chapter suggests, there may be quali-

tative differences in learning, resulting from improved planning and teaching, which do not lead to quantitative gains on criterion scores used to date; the learning which does occur perhaps is more relevant to the needs of the learner than those outcomes reported herein.

3. The weaknesses in the studies to be presented here should provide clues leading to improved studies of similar types in the future; i.e., longitudinal studies using more sophisticated measures of achievement. These studies would have widespread potential for education as is indicated in Chapter V.

Resource Guides and Critical Thinking[1]

Of the several general goals of education, critical thinking behaviors stand high on the list of those which the school should foster, in the view of many people. Unfortunately, many of the standard teaching procedures emphasize behaviors which tend toward convergent thinking (i.e., focusing on one single response to a situation or problem) and away from divergent thinking (i.e., examining many different alternative solutions to problems). To foster critical thinking, objectives of both types, in addition to others associated with this skill, must be emphasized.

Because the use of computer assisted planning for the generation of resource guides facilitates the selection of objectives related to critical thinking, and also because this technique provides for individualized approaches to the acquisition of this skill, there should be a relationship between the use of resource guides and the attainment of these objectives.

In brief, do students whose teachers use resource guides do better on a test of critical thinking than do students whose teachers do not use resource guides? Do those students whose teachers use resource guides with only objectives related to critical thinking do better on a test of this skill than do those who use resource guides without objectives directly related to this skill? Further, is there a greater variance of scores on a test of critical thinking when a resource guide is used, giving evidence of more individualization of instruction?

This study used a pre- and post-test of the *Watson-Glaser Critical Thinking Appraisal* to compare scores of students whose teachers used resource guides with critical thinking objectives only, students whose teachers used resource guides without critical thinking objectives, and students whose teachers did not use resource guides but were provided with simulated materials. All three groups were instructed on the unit *U.S. Constitution* for the tenth grade. In addition to comparing overall scores on the above test, subtest scores on inference, recognition of assumptions, deduction, interpretation, and evaluation of arguments were compared.

The analysis of covariance was used to compare scores

on the total test and the subtests. The Scheffé test of multiple comparisons was used to locate significant differences between groups. An F test of variance ratio was used to compare range of scores on pre- and post-tests for each group.

Adjusted mean score differences favored students in classrooms where teachers used resource guides with critical thinking objectives over those using resource guides without critical thinking objectives and those not using resource guides. These differences were not significant at the .05 level of confidence and, hence, no appreciable gains were inferred. In short, at the time of the study, no relationship was shown between use of the resource guide and student achievement of skills of critical thinking.

An analysis of variance ratios of scores for the three groups shows that those groups whose teachers used resource guides had a considerably greater range of scores than did the group whose teachers used the simulated materials. This indication of greater range in scores (dispersion from the mean) without any significant loss in mean scores may indicate that the greatest benefit which may accrue from the use of resource guides is to facilitate greater variability in learning without suffering significant losses in overall achievement of skills of critical thinking.

Resource Guides and Attitudes Toward Mathematics[2]

The development of positive student attitudes toward mathematics is also an important educational goal. Theory suggests that the curriculum preplanning practices of the teacher can foster desirable attitudes by the selection of teaching-learning situations specifically oriented toward attitude development, and by arranging learning experiences based upon individual students' learning characteristics. The computer-based resource guide should facilitate the formation of desirable attitudes because the guide supplies the teacher with preplanning suggestions per specific goal and per individual learner variables.

This study was designed to determine experimentally whether the computer-based resource guide helps the teacher to prepare a written preplanned unit of mathematics instruction and whether these learning experiences arranged with the aid of the guide do affect more positive student attitudes toward mathematics.

As regards preplanning skills, each of four criteria indicative of a good unit of instruction appeared more often in the plans of teachers who used a guide to preplan than in the plans of teachers who used a standard resource unit, as determined by a jury of qualified educators. When quantified, the average of the jurists' ratings from the guide group's plans was greater than the corresponding figure for the unit group's plans for each of the four criteria. In all cases, these differences were statistically significant at the .05 level.

With respect to student attitudes, those classroom units whose teachers selected instructional objectives specifically designed to attain positive attitudes toward mathematics, and whose learning experiences were preplanned with the aid of a guide, achieved greater average attitude measures on a subject preference index, the Aiken scale, and the Dutton scale. Though these trends were consistent, statistically significant differences were not achieved at the .05 level.

In the preparation of a written preplanned unit of mathematics instruction, teachers aided in preplanning by a guide exercised a greater degree of decision making skill in four facets of the preplanning process: teacher choice of learning experiences per each particular objective to be attained, teacher provision for appropriate small-group and individual instruction, teacher organization of a developmental sequence of unit learning experiences, and teacher selection of an appropriate variety of unit learning experiences.

With respect to student attitudes toward mathematics, the trends favored classroom units whose instructional goals were attitude oriented and whose learning experiences were preplanned by teachers using a guide, but conclusive evidence regarding these trends will require further study.

To obtain more conclusive evidence concerning attitude development, a modified replication of this study should consider: (1) a random sample of large size, (2) the individual student as the unit for statistical inference, (3) an extended treatment exposure to include several units over at least a semester's time duration, (4) provision to secure all requested instructional materials, (5) the sole use of teachers who are experienced in unit planning and teaching, (6) a group without any preplanning aid for contrast, and (7) a multivariate statistical analysis of a number of attitude measures in addition to a general liking for mathematics.

Resource Guides and Understanding[3]

The teaching and measuring of learning objectives related to understanding has become a major concern in education. The term "understanding" has become common in educational circles. Seldom can we examine a list of objectives in a unit or lesson plan without encountering the words "understanding," "comprehension," or their equivalent. The purpose of this study was to determine the effectiveness of the resource guide in areas related to understanding.

Planning with a resource guide was compared to planning with a resource unit in regard to effective teaching for understanding. The comparisons made between the unit and the guide were relative to the differences which resulted on a measure of understanding related to a teaching unit on *Transportation.* The mean scores of pupils taught by teachers using the resource guide were compared with the mean scores of pupils taught by teachers using the resource unit.

Fifteen classes were selected and divided into three stratified treatment groups, each of which contained five classes. Two classes in each of the three groups were from suburban schools, two from urban schools, and one from a rural school district.

One group consisted of five classes whose teachers used a resource guide with objectives of understanding. Another group consisted of five classes whose teachers used a resource guide without objectives of understanding. The third group consisted of five classes whose teachers used a resource unit.

The test used in this study was designed by the investigator and measured understanding-type objectives related to the unit *Transportation.* Validity and reliability were determined after intensive testing, retesting and revision. The Kuder-Richardson formula was used to determine reliability. An item analysis was also made. The investigator was concerned with two questions:

1. Will there be a significant difference in the mean scores on a measure of understanding, related to transportation, among pupils whose teachers used the resource guide with objectives of understanding, pupils whose teachers used a resource guide without objectives of understanding, and pupils whose teachers used a resource unit?

2. Will there be a significant difference in the mean scores on a measure of understanding related to transportation between pupils who are taught by means of a resource guide and those who are taught by means of the resource unit?

Although the differences among mean scores for the three groups were not significant at the .05 level of confidence, the investigator makes note of the following:

1. Pupils taught by teachers who used the resource guide with objectives of understanding achieved greater gains in mean scores on a test of understandings in transportation than those pupils taught by teachers who used a resource guide without objectives of understanding and those taught by teachers using a simple resource unit.

2. Pupils taught by teachers who used the resource guide without objectives of understanding achieved greater gains in mean scores on a test of understandings in transportation than those pupils taught by teachers using a resource unit.

3. With regard to "comprehension" type objectives, a teacher's decisions regarding these objectives tend to have a strong influence on pupil achievement. In this study, pupils taught by teachers using the resource guide as an aid achieved understandings which resulted in learnings that enabled them to better translate, interpret, and extrapolate information related to the study of transportation.

Resource Guides and Knowledge of Specifics[4]

The final study to be discussed in this chapter examined the effects of using computer assisted planning on the attainment of the objectives long held to be the central task of the school, those of factual recall or knowledge of specific facts and information. These objectives will continue to be of major importance because it is recognized that in order for more complex cognitive processes, as well as affective and psychomotor ones, to occur there must be knowledge.

Since individuals vary in the storehouse of knowledge which they possess, an individualized program of instruction would seem to permit students to begin with their present competencies and progress farther than they could in a non-individualized program. Further, such a program should facilitate the learning of more incidental facts by permitting students to branch away from the central theme of the study.

This study sought to discover whether students whose teachers used resource guides would show a greater gain on a standardized test of factual recall related to the unit, *U.S. Constitution,* than would students whose teachers did not utilize resource guides. Also, this study inquired into the possibility that students whose teachers used resource guides would show greater achievement on tests only vaguely related to the topic, *U.S. Constitution,* and on test items least related to the topic according to expert judges.

Scores on the Science Research Associates' Test on *Principles of Democracy* were used as items closely related to the central theme of the unit, and scores on selected subtests of Magruder's *Tests on American Governments* were used as items away from the central theme. These scores were compared with an analysis of variance and Bartlett's test for homogeneity of variance.

Results show that neither group achieved significantly

greater scores on the test related to the central theme of the study. Taking into consideration the fact that in fourteen out of twenty-one of the subtests only items vaguely related and least related to the central theme significantly favored the groups whose teachers used resource guides makes this finding important. It tends to suggest that without appreciable loss of achievement related to the central theme, gains were made by the experimental groups on items not so directly related to this theme.

Conclusion

Those studies reported above are restricted to a few specific goals of the school. These studies focused on instructional objectives of critical thinking, attitudes toward mathematics, understanding, and knowledge of specifics. In the main, the studies reported a lack of significant differences between comparison groups.

The lack of statistical significance between groups highlights one major conclusion: the use of resource guides has not resulted in *lower* achievement on the specific objectives studied. The gains which were reported, therefore, are on the positive side and are, at least, encouraging. These beneficial effects which appear related to the use of resource guides are, in brief, that more individualization of instruction occurs, permitting greater individual expression of achievement; that teacher preplanning skills are improved; that teacher decision making relative to preplanning is improved; that students achieve greater gains on skills of understanding enabling them to better translate, interpret, and extrapolate; and that students acquire knowledge over and above that related to the central theme of a unit to a greater degree. In addition, the findings reported in the next chapter on instructional behavior must be considered in light of these studies.

References

1. Eisele, James E. "Using Resource Guides to Teach the Skills of Critical Thinking," Unpublished Dissertation, State University of New York at Buffalo.
2. Young, James. "The Use of a Computer Based Resource Guide to Preplan a Unit of Instruction and to Develop Student Attitudes Toward Mathematics," Unpublished Dissertation, State University of New York at Buffalo.
3. Licata, William. "The Resource Guide as an Aid for the Teaching of Understanding," Unpublished Dissertation, State University of New York at Buffalo.
4. Hicken, James E. "An Experimental Analysis of the Effects on Pupil Achievement of Using an Electronic Information Retrieval System in Unit Teaching," Unpublished Dissertation, State University of New York at Buffalo.

CHAPTER IV

COMPUTER ASSISTED PLANNING
AND INSTRUCTIONAL BEHAVIOR*

One of the basic goals of curriculum planning is the improvement of instruction. This improvement of instruction hinges on the ability of the professional classroom teacher to make the right decision at the right time in planning and executing a teaching-learning situation for individual children. John Goodlad writes:

> The right decision at the right moment is the essence of good teaching. Right decisions are those that time learning perfectly for the individual student. A series of such decisions moves the

* This chapter was written by **Thomas J. Clayback.**

student forward at an optimum pace. Obviously, such timing and pacing are no more accidental than is the perfect catch by the professional outfielder. They are, indeed, complex but they can also be acquired. They are attainable only through the dedicated application of a reasonable amount of intelligence, especially in planning. Acquisition of teaching lore is no guarantee of good timing and pacing in teaching, but good teaching is not possible without it.[1]

The previous chapter discussed some of the actual and potential effects of computer assisted planning of instruction upon student behavior. In essence, as pointed out by Goodlad, whatever changes in student behavior may occur are the result of teachers making the right decision at the right moment. The changes in student behavior associated with the utilization of computer assisted planning occur not so much as a direct effect of the resulting plans for individualizing instruction, but as a result of the improvements which these procedures are able to foster in teacher decision making.

A few investigations have begun to examine the value of computer assisted planning to facilitate and improve the decisions and instructional behavior of classroom teachers. Some impressive data are slowly emerging which support Goodlad's thesis that desirable teaching behaviors can be acquired, and the data suggest that computer assisted planning may provide greater impetus and support for their acquisition. This chapter presents the findings of research in four areas of teacher functions: first, the functions associated with preplanning of instruction are considered; next, some aspects of instructional behavior during the execution of teaching-learning plans are taken into account; third, processes associated with the selection of instructional objectives are examined; and, finally, the planning and implementation functions of teachers working in a team arrangement are looked at. These four areas represent four respective studies which have been completed to date; more are in process and still more will follow in the future.

Preplanning

As already indicated, a major goal of computer assisted planning is to improve instruction by helping classroom teachers make more and better decisions in preplanning teaching-learning situations. Goldberg[2] inquired into three aspects of instructional decision making in order to determine if these functions were facilitated through the use of computer generated resource guides. Her concern was with the time dimension of preplanning for instruction, the quality of the resulting plans, and subsequent changes in instructional behavior in the classroom.

Goldberg used teacher-kept time logs of various tasks associated with preplanning, teacher prepared outlines of the planned units of instruction, and trained observers using a specially adapted classroom observation instrument[3] for comparing experimental and control groups, randomly assigned, on the three issues cited above.

On the time dimension Goldberg discovered that teachers using computer generated plans required considerably more time for subsequent preplanning than did those not using the experimental print-outs. Analysis of the teacher-kept time logs revealed that the additional time requirement was related to the nature of the preplanning tasks. Teachers using the computer generated plans devoted their preplanning time to tasks more closely allied to individualizing instruction than did the other teachers. Certainly, planning for individualized instruction requires more time than planning to teach for the same objectives for all students in the same way. One conclusion which can be drawn from Goldberg's study is that the assistance which teachers receive from the experimental materials encourages and facilitates the making of decisions for the individualization of instruction—which otherwise *may not even be attempted.*

The written plans of teachers using the resource guides also exceeded those of the other teachers in overall quality. The execution of these plans was also deemed superior for the experimental teachers. Goldberg reported the results of using trained observers before and after the planning and implementation of instructional units as favoring the experimental teachers in the acquisition of several dimensions of desirable teaching behavior.

Instructional Behavior

Changes in instructional behavior were reported by Goldberg as one aspect of a study dealing primarily with preplanning. Holden[4] used the same observation instrument as Goldberg to examine more intensively any instructional behavior changes resulting from the utilization of computer assisted planning. Holden's study addressed several aspects of instructional behavior associated with executing plans for individualized instruction. These behaviors included the encouragement of independent thinking in students, the creation of an atmosphere of accepting individuality in the classroom, the appropriate selection and use of instructional materials, the appropriate selection and use of instructional methods, the use of challenge as a motivator, and sensitivity to the needs of individuals.

Holden found considerable evidence that teachers using the computer-based materials have increased in both number and quality of observed incidents on all of the above dimensions which exceeded those of the control groups. In addition, he found the use of a wider variety of instructional materials and greater use of individual and small-group methods, with concomitant reduction in large-group activities, among the teachers using the experimental materials.

In sum, this study reports that the use of computer generated resource guides are highly correlated with changes in the following instructional behaviors:

1. Encouraging pupils to engage in independent

thinking;

2. Creating an accepting atmosphere in the classroom;
3. Making appropriate selection and use of instructional materials;
4. Making appropriate selection and use of teaching methods;
5. Motivating pupils through challenge without threat;
6. Employing a wider variety of instructional materials;
7. Using a greater number of individual and small-group methods of teaching, and fewer large-group methods; and,
8. Encouraging more pupil involvement and interaction.

Team Teaching

Many of the obstacles to effective decision making about individualized instruction by a single classroom teacher also encroach upon the decision making of teachers working in teams. The individual plans provided by the computer which seem to assist individual teachers seem even more uniquely suited to team teaching arrangements because the differentiated instructional procedures for individual students suggest differentiated staff responsibilities, the crux of most team teaching plans. Whether or not resource guides could be employed effectively in this kind of arrangement was the subject of a study by McMahon.[5]

McMahon reports a case study of an entire staff in a suburban elementary school organized into instructional teams. The teachers in this experiment were given computer plans to assist in the preparation of a program of individualized instruction. Data were collected through the use of logs, interviews, and questionnaires to examine and analyze the use of the provided materials by the teams for planning and implementing the resulting plans.

The study reported that teachers did, in fact, use the guides to plan all the elements of a teaching-learning situation. In addition, McMahon states that the guides served as a basis for cooperative planning between teachers and between both teachers and pupils. He further concluded that the use of resource guides affects the team teachers' knowledge and conception of individualized instruction and unit teaching, as well as improving the specificity with which they identify learner characteristics which are relevant to the creation of individualized instructional plans.

Selection of Objectives

In terms of deriving maximum benefits from the use of computer assisted planning for the individualization of instruction, Bianchi[6] and Burr[7] studied the effects of involving students in the process of selecting their own instructional objectives. More specifically, Bianchi examined the differences which existed among objectives *selected* by teachers, by students, and cooperatively, and differences between objectives *formulated* by teachers and by students. Burr looked at the effects on the planned teaching-learning situation of involving students in the process of selecting objectives for a computer print-out.

Bianchi analyzed different sets of instructional objectives which were derived through selection from existing lists stored in computer memory banks and through original formulation by teachers alone, by students alone, and cooperatively by both. His comparisons revealed that there were, in fact, considerable differences between the resulting sets of objectives. Students both selected and wrote objectives which were more concerned with personal problems and concerns than were those selected or written by teachers. Comparison between objectives which teachers deem interesting and important for individuals and those which the individual students identified as such showed little similarity. Through cooperative planning, however, these differences were nearly all ameliorated and students were guided to write objectives which reflected a wide range of cognitive processes.

Burr used objective test scores, a count of objectives selected, and interviews with teachers and students to ascertain the effects of student participation in the objective selection process. With regard to the objectives, themselves,

Burr discovered that those selected cooperatively better matched the interests of the students, contained a higher percentage of affective objectives and a lower percentage of cognitive recall objectives, and were more unique to each individual than were those selected by teachers alone.

Burr also found that this cooperative planning resulted in greater learning in similar amounts of time in spite of the fact that the cooperative planning groups spent part of the instructional time in planning activities. The preplanning time of the experimental teachers exceeded that of teachers who selected objectives without direct student involvement. Another of Burr's conclusions needs to be quoted in full. He states that when students and teachers cooperatively select instructional objectives:

> The individualization of instruction occurs to a greater degree. Teachers involve students in planning other parts of the teaching-learning situation, tend to act as guides rather than as presenters of information, do more preplanning, and do more planning with individual objectives, agree more often with the teacher on an end-of-unit grade, and are more aware of the influence of their studies on their selection of everyday activities.

Conclusion

There are beginning to emerge many fascinating implications for teacher behavior of using the assistance of plans generated by computers to individualize instruction. Perhaps prophetically, Goldberg showed that teachers will spend considerably more time in planning for individualized instruction when given choices about which decisions can be made. It appears that this additional time is worthwhile in terms of improvements in instructional behavior which occur both to individual teachers and to teachers working in teams.

These conclusions, along with others drawn by the researchers, point to the use of computer assisted planning activities as a valuable aid to inservice training of teachers. Of course, more information is needed but, at present, the studies seem to indicate that these activities have some remarkable effects on instructional behavior.

Vastly more information of the type offered by Burr and Bianchi is also needed, although they have begun to scratch the surface of identifying practices which optimize the utilization of computer assisted planning. Other studies,[8],[9] less directly related to teacher instructional behavior, may shed additional light on this area and many, many more are needed.

References

1. Goodlad, John I. *School, Curriculum and the Individual.* Waltham, Massachusetts: Blaisdell Publishing Company, 1966, 208.
2. Goldberg, Minerva J. "Using a Resource Guide to Preplan a Unit of Instruction," Unpublished Doctoral Dissertation, State University of New York at Buffalo,

Buffalo, N.Y., 1966.

3.   Jason, Hilliard. "An Analysis of Teaching Practices at Seven Selected American Medical Schools," Unpublished Doctoral Dissertation, University of Buffalo, Buffalo, N.Y., 1961.

4.   Holden, George. "Changes in Instructional Behavior of Non-Unit Teaching Teachers When Resource Guides Are Used," Unpublished Doctoral Dissertation, State University of New York at Buffalo, Buffalo, New York, 1966.

5.   McMahon, Edward James. "Using a Computer Generated Resource Guide to Plan for and Implement Individualization of Instruction in a Team Teaching Arrangement," Unpublished Doctoral Dissertation, State University of New York at Buffalo, Buffalo, New York, 1970.

6.   Bianchi, Gordon B. "A Descriptive Comparison of the Differences Among Instructional Objectives Which Are Formulated and Selected With and Without the Participation of Students," Unpublished Doctoral Dissertation, State University of New York at Buffalo, Buffalo, New York, 1970.

7.   Burr, Bruce D. "Student Participation in the Selection of Instructional Objectives for a Computer Resource Guide Which Teachers Use to Preplan the Individualization of Instruction," Unpublished Doctoral Dissertation, State University of New York at Buffalo, Buffalo, New York, 1971.

8.   Sauter, Robert C. "Effect of Dissimilar Combinations of Learner Variables on Learner Achievement Through Utilization of an Electronic Data Processing Equipment Resource Guide," Unpublished Doctoral Dissertation, State University of New York at Buffalo, Buffalo, New York, 1970.

9. O'Neil, Elizabeth S. "Teacher Use of Pupil Affect in Planning Small Group Activities for a Speaking and Listening Unit," Unpublished Doctoral Dissertation, State University of New York at Buffalo, Buffalo, New York, 1971.

CHAPTER V

COMPUTER ASSISTED PLANNING AS A VEHICLE FOR CURRICULUM EVALUATION AND RESEARCH*

The intent of this chapter is to describe how the unique characteristics of computer-based resource units (also referred to as computer assisted planning) lend themselves to a wide variety of curriculum research and evaluation strategies.

The development of computer-based resource units is based on the concept that electronic data processing equipment can be applied in such a way as to relate preplanning of a teaching-learning situation to the needs and receptive

---

*This chapter is based upon a paper by **Gordon Bianchi** and **Bruce D. Burr** read at the 1970 AERA Meeting, Minneapolis, Minnesota, March 5-6, 1970.

abilities of individual pupils. In constructing computer-based resource units, groups of interested and expert teachers formulate measurable objectives around a center of interest or unit of instruction such as "The Solar System" or "News Media Analysis." Next, they designate content, select pertinent materials, and devise instructional activities and evaluation devices. All of the above-mentioned components are eventually coded to one or a number of the objectives in the resource unit.

A cross coding process is then utilized to relate these teaching-learning components (objectives, content, activities, materials, and evaluation devices) to various learner variables (introductory activity, developmental activity, etc.).

In cooperation with the teacher, the student selects objectives relevant to his own felt needs and interests, and supplies the necessary information related to his own learner characteristics or variables. Subsequently, the individual student receives a personally tailored curriculum guide related to a particular unit of study. Concurrently, the teacher receives a similar guide for the total class, consisting of objectives which are considered relevant to the needs and interests of all students in the class. Each objective in these "personal" or "total class" resource guides is matched to numerous items of content, activities, materials, and measuring devices.

By providing a variety of suggestions for each objective, the user, whether teacher or student, still has considerable latitude in determining how the objectives will be achieved. In other words, *ultimate teaching-learning decisions are made by people, not by computers.*

Vehicle for Research and Evaluation

Although the primary purpose of computer assisted planning is the individualization of instruction, the systematic control afforded by the computer over teaching-learning components and over student variables has resulted in an exceptionally valuable medium for curriculum research and evaluation—with virtually limitless possibilities.

There is no attempt being made to conclude that research and evaluation conducted through the use of computer assisted planning would be otherwise impossible. Indeed, there is nothing described here which cannot be accomplished solely with the use of human resources. On the other hand, the unique characteristics of computer assisted planning, and the efficient method of processing information by computer, result in a systematically consistent process with a potential for research which is limited only by the imagination of the user. Additionally, this procedure will save literally millions of man hours for curriculum researchers.

The remainder of this chapter will describe more specifically some of these unique characteristics of computer-based resource units, or computer assisted planning. Brief descriptions of completed studies, studies in progress and potential studies will be utilized as examples.

The information stored in a computer-based resource unit is organized around the components of the teaching-learning situation and is coded for retrieval to a set of learner variables and professional variables. These components and variables are often considerations in educational research and, therefore, the computer-based resource unit becomes an effective tool in research and evaluation.

The objectives component for a computer-based resource unit has facilitated two recent studies (see previous chapter). Bianchi[1] used the objectives component from two units to determine what differences existed when students participated with teachers in the selection and formulation of instructional objectives for a unit of study. The objectives from the units, "American People" and "Drugs and Narcotics," were used as examples of teacher formulated objectives. The investigator asked students to formulate instructional objectives which were then compared with the teacher formulated objectives from the unit.

In another study, Burr[2] used the objectives component of a unit to determine effects of student participation in the selection of objectives from a unit which teachers used in preplanning and teaching. Teachers alone and teachers with students made selections from among the given objectives. Among other effects, the amount of student participation in planning other components of the teaching-learning situation was studied.

Computer assisted planning can also be used to isolate a learner variable or a cluster of learner variables to determine the effect of these variables. In a recent study, Sauter[3] isolated the variables of I.Q., social class, interests, and developmental tasks in an effort to compare the suggestions for the components of the teaching-learning situation made by teachers with those in computer produced resource guides. Some of the resource guides used in this comparison were produced using each of the above variables alone, and other guides were produced using all four of the variables.

Both the components of the teaching-learning situation and learner variables in a computer-based resource unit can be combined to study areas such as critical thinking and understanding. Eisele[4] studied the difference in the skills of critical thinking among students whose teachers used a resource guide or unit. Eisele isolated the "critical thinking" objectives in a unit so that one treatment group received a guide containing only objectives and suggestions related to "critical thinking." Another treatment received a guide containing the "non-critical thinking" objectives and suggestions in the entire resource unit. Licata[5] followed a similar procedure in his study of understanding by isolating the "understanding" objectives in the resource unit on *Transportation.*

Computer assisted planning also provides a vehicle for the study of teacher behavior, particularly when aspects of unit teaching and planning are being compared. Holden,[6] for example, investigated the use of the concept as an inservice aid by furnishing one set of teachers a resource guide to plan their unit of instruction. These teachers were compared with another set who received no computer materials to aid them in planning.

Teachers' behaviors were compared as to use of instructional materials, reaction to pupils' needs, and attitude toward students among several factors measured. Goldberg[7] compared the planning decisions of teachers who received a resource unit. For each group, Goldberg studied certain observable behaviors of teachers, time spent in planning, and the degree to which individual activities were planned and individual materials provided to individual students.

Two characteristics of the computer assisted planning provide additional important research advantages. The first is the variety of grade levels and subject areas which are incorporated in the existing units. Presently, over thirty units of instruction have been created. They include a wide range of subject areas and topics relevant to general and special education for groups ranging from preschoolers up to and including college students. This condition will permit the researcher, regardless of his subject matter or grade level expertise, to select that discipline and that age range with which he is most knowledgeable and in which he is most interested.

The second characteristic concerns the invariability of format of the computer-based resource units. Regardless of the subject or grade level of the unit, the format is always uniform, consisting as it does of suggested teaching-learning components which are generated as a result of combinations of student variables. This characteristic of "format consistency" is of singular advantage to the researcher who wishes to replicate a study at a different time, or at a different grade level, or with a different subject area. In addition, both experimental and control groups would receive essentially identical resource guides in terms of format, even though one of the variables, I.Q. for example, might serve as a screen for the components of the control group but not for the experimental group. This situation would tend to minimize any Hawthorne Effect.

Research in Progress

A brief description of a few studies in progress which are utilizing computer-based resource units as a research tool, wholly or in part, will illustrate other possibilities.

Ordinarily, instructional objectives are considered tools for preplanning unit strategies. O'Connell,[8] utilizing the third-grade unit, *Communities of Man,* is attempting to determine a dynamic role for instructional objectives during the actual teaching-learning process.

Koenig,[9] in studying the effects of individualized reading activities on science achievement, is utilizing the large-group, small-group, non-reading and reading activities related to a fifth grade resource guide on *The Solar System.*

Bartoo[10] is gathering data on teacher decision making related to the in-school and out-of-school activities of students. In order to provide all of the participating teachers and students with the same general orientation to unit teaching, each class initially will be provided any resource guide it desires. Thereafter, all experimental groups will receive the *Speaking and Listening* guide.

O'Neil[11] is using the unit on *Speaking and Listening* to determine how an intermediate level teacher deals with affect in planning small-group activities. Containing over 200 small-group activities and nearly 150 affective and cognitive objectives, this unit will serve as a convenient experimental tool.

Teacher and Teacher Training Assessment

An area with considerable research and evaluation potential concerns an assessment of the abilities of teachers to formulate high quality objectives, activities, content and measuring devices.

Without extensive probing, certain trends are becoming apparent to those individuals who have been involved in the production and distribution of computer-based resource units. A few of these trends are:

1. Teachers have not developed a great deal of skill in writing objectives which involve the "Application"[12] of skills

and concepts.

2. Teachers have not developed a great deal of skill in writing creative and/or original measuring devices.

3. Teachers have not developed a great deal of skill in prescribing instructional activities for exceptional students.

4. Teachers have difficulty designating the extent to which certain instructional activities, evaluation devices, etc., are more appropriate for boys or for girls.

The implications of these trends are obvious as they would apply to research and to evaluation of teaching and teacher training.

Conclusion

This chapter described ways in which the unique characteristics of computer assisted planning lend themselves to curriculum research and evaluation strategies by providing a systematic and consistent vehicle for controlling variables, particularly those related to the teaching-learning situation and learner characteristics. Several completed and ongoing studies are presented to cite examples of ways in which these unique characteristics have been used, to illustrate the potential of the process, and to suggest other possibilities for further curriculum research and evaluation.

References

1. Bianchi, Gordon. "A Descriptive Comparison of the Differences Among Instructional Objectives Which Are

Formulated and Selected With and Without the Participation of Students," Unpublished Doctoral Dissertation, State University of New York at Buffalo, 1970.

2. Burr, Bruce D. "The Participation of Students in the Selection of Objectives for a Computer Generated Resource Guide," Unpublished Doctoral Dissertation, State University of New York at Buffalo, 1971.

3. Sauter, Robert. "Effect of Dissimilar Combinations of Learner Variables on Learner Achievement Through Utilization of an Electronic Data Processing Equipment Resource Guide," Unpublished Doctoral Dissertation, State University of New York at Buffalo, 1970.

4. Eisele, James E. "Using a Resource Guide to Develop the Skills of Critical Thinking," Unpublished Doctoral Dissertation, State University of New York at Buffalo, 1966.

5. Licata, William. "The Resource Guide as an Aid for the Teaching of Understanding," Unpublished Doctoral Dissertation, State University of New York at Buffalo, 1969.

6. Holden, George. "Changes in Instructional Behavior of Non-Unit Teaching Teachers When Resource Guides Are Used," Unpublished Doctoral Dissertation, State University of New York at Buffalo, 1966.

7. Goldberg, Minerva J. "Using a Resource Guide to Preplan a Unit of Instruction," Unpublished Doctoral Dissertation, State University of New York at Buffalo, 1966.

8. O'Connell, Joseph. "A Study of Instructional Objectives as Related to the Dynamics of the Teaching-Learning Situation," Doctoral Dissertation in Progress, State University of New York at Buffalo.

9. Koenig, Herbert. "The Effect of Individualized Reading Activities on Science Achievement," Doctoral Disser-

tation in Progress, State University of New York at Buffalo.

10. Bartoo, Eugene. "Instructional Decisions Related to the Interests of Emerging Adolescents," Doctoral Dissertation in Progress, State University of New York at Buffalo.

11. O'Neil, Elizabeth. "Teacher Use of Pupil Affect in Planning Small Group Activities for a Speaking and Listening Unit," Doctoral Dissertation in Progress, State University of New York at Buffalo.

12. Bloom, Benjamin S. (ed.) *The Classification of Educational Goals, Handbook I: Cognitive Domain.* New York: David McKay Company, Inc., 1956.

CHAPTER VI

UTILIZATION AND IMPLICATIONS OF COMPUTER ASSISTED PLANNING OF CURRICULUM AND INSTRUCTION

Efforts to improve curriculum and instruction cannot possibly be successful without moving beyond research and development such as is described in preceding chapters. In order to realize success these efforts and their vast potential must be known about by the many people involved in the educational enterprise, and the proposed changes in present practice must have widespread adoption.

Guba, in his model of the change process, which includes the steps of research, development, diffusion, and adoption, has this to say about diffusion and adoption:

The most potent solutions that man can devise to

overcome his problems have little utility if prac-
titioners know little about them or have little
opportunity to discover how the solutions work.
The purpose of diffusion is to create awareness and
provide opportunities for the assessment of the
invention. Diffusion, in short, makes the invention
available and understandable to the practitioner.

And,

Adapting an invention to the local situation and
installing it are the purposes of adoption. Such
activity presents many difficulties. Every situation
has its own peculiarities; thus, an invention cannot
simply be slipped into place without considerable
modification to itself, to the system, or to both. A
prudent local administrator should test the innovation before assimilating it as a component part of
his system. This assimilation may involve training
local personnel, arranging appropriate scheduling,
modifying available space, and the like. The adoption process, therefore, establishes the invention as
part of the ongoing program and, in time, converts
it into a "non-innovation."[1]

This chapter is devoted to the facilitation of diffusion
and adoption of procedures for computer assisted planning of
curriculum and instruction. Because much information about
the process is already provided in preceding chapters, this
chapter will center first on the utilization of these procedures
in school situations. Then, to further augment diffusion, this
chapter will explore several of the many implications
inherent in computer assisted planning, some of which have
been touched upon briefly in preceding chapters.

Utilization

The question to be addressed in this section is, "How does a school district, a school, or a classroom teacher or group of teachers go about using computer assisted planning?" The answer is at once both simple and complex. The use of computer assisted planning is a simple undertaking because there is a data base for the use of resource guides which exists almost for the asking. On the other hand, utilization is complex because, as pointed out by Guba," . . . an invention cannot simply be slipped into place without considerable modification to itself, to the system, or both."[2] Fortunately, some of the complexities of adoption are reduced by the very flexible nature of the invention itself, in this particular case.

In order to describe ways in which computer assisted planning might be utilized, a continuum can be conceptualized from the simple to the complex. In reality, the degree of complexity will vary from one situation to the next; there are an infinite number of levels of complexity which may appear on the continuum. For convenience, three hypothetical points on this continuum will be identified and described, with examples where appropriate. The points to be described will be labeled, simply, first, second, and third levels—from simple to complex, respectively.

First Level Utilization

Somewhere on the least complex end of the continuum would fall the first level of utilization. In fact, this may be the most simple of all possible applications of computer assisted planning.

At this level a potential user merely follows the procedures set forth under the section on implementation in Chapter II. That is, he requests from one of the service centers* a unit from the listing in Appendix B.

After receiving a user's packet from the service agency, the requestor selects objectives for the total class and for each individual in the class, and completes a Learner Variable sheet for each student. When these items are returned to the servicing agency, the computer performs the following functions, as described by Harnack, and returns the results to the user.

In sum, the electronic computer can perform the three functions in this context:

1) Responding to the learning objectives identified by the teacher and/or pupils, it can provide an appropriate content (subject matter) outline.

2) By taking into consideration the variables of learning objectives and the characteristic composition of the class, it can suggest:

   a) significant large-group activities;

   b) significant small-group activities;

---

* At present the most likely source of service can be found at the Center for Curriculum Planning, 220A Foster Hall, State University of New York at Buffalo, Buffalo, New York, and the Board of Cooperative Educational Services, 99 Aero Drive, Buffalo, New York.

      c)   significant instructional materials for the total group; and

      d)   significant measuring devices for the total group.

   3)   By taking into consideration the variables of learning objectives and the characteristics of each learner, it can suggest suitable instructional material and individual activities for each student, per each objective chosen.[3]

Generally speaking, no more than 48 hours time is consumed between the receipt of the completed forms at the service agency and the mailing of the complete resource guide. Far less time is necessary for the actual generation of a guide, which is accomplished usually within minutes or even seconds. However, the potential user, even at this level of utilization, is cautioned to place his requests sufficiently in advance of the time for actual usage to allow one week for delivery and two more weeks for subsequent planning.

Utilization at this level may require some adaptation of both the invention and the using system to achieve maximum success. Changes required in computer assisted planning are relatively easy to make, flexibility being a major virtue of the program. Users can and must make numerous decisions, anyway, and can almost design their own unique application by selection of units, print-out format, objectives, professional decision variables and learner variables. Further, the use of any or all parts of any print-out is optional and can be adapted to a local situation. For example, one teacher may choose to emphasize content while another relies more heavily on activities. Innumerable combinations are possible. Of course, the using teacher is encouraged to provide feedback data, which contribute directly to the updating of the data base.

Changes in the user's system may not come so easily. Findings of a recent evaluation of this kind of utilization indicate that there seem to be at least two major problems which might be prevented within the using system. These are 1) the lack of adequate instructional materials as specified in computer generated print-outs (this includes poor physical facilities) and 2) the need for greater assistance in interpreting and using the print-outs.[4] With adequate planning these problems could be eliminated by supportive staffs of using schools.

These findings have been corroborated in countless situations. Recently, the senior author worked closely with teachers in Atlanta, Georgia, and discovered similar problems. In this case, certain specific forms of needed assistance became evident. These included the need for released time for planning, the need for location and acquisition of instructional materials, and instructional and clerical assistance so that the teacher may work more directly with individuals and small groups.

Despite the problems, first level utilization can be beneficial. Evidence of the advantages are found in the research reported previously as well as in the day-by-day experiences of those who employ computer assisted planning of curriculum and instruction.

Second Level Utilization

A second level of utilization would be both more complex and more comprehensive. It would be more complex in the sense that more changes in the user system would undoubtedly be required for optimum use. It would be more comprehensive in that more people and parts of the system would be involved in the utilization of computer assisted planning. Further, it is conceivable that different applications of the process, in addition to the use of resource guides, would be employed at this level. Essentially, this level would include two components, service and development.

Service

Service consists of providing teachers with the necessary data for decision making. Even at this level, this could be handled through an existing service agency as described above. However, for greater economy and more flexibility, the user at this level would be wise to obtain the data bank and programs for equipment in his immediate locale. The cost of such acquisition is negligible since no charge is made for the information stored and only the cost of tape and a small service charge for duplication is incurred.

Coordination is definitely required at this level of

utilization, as is computer programming support. Other forms of supportive assistance may be equally desirable. Curriculum specialists, teacher aides and assistants, librarians, and media utilization experts can greatly enhance the value of computer assisted planning. This is especially important at this level of utilization to avoid frustrating large numbers of potential users through poor usage.

In addition to the normal generation of resource guides for classroom use, activities at this level may include inservice education, curriculum analysis, adapting the data base for special needs, media utilization studies, and special projects. Each of these requires brief explanation. Of course, other activities may be devised as may be appropriate.

Inservice Education. At this level, the using system may train its own personnel in both the use of computer assisted planning and as consultants to others wishing to use such approaches to the individualization of instruction. No specific procedures for this activity are recommended, although it will probably be necessary for some local school personnel to be trained at one of the existing service agencies.

Curriculum Analysis. Through specially written programs, print-outs can be generated in various forms to reveal information about the scope and sequence of the curriculum. For example, one program provides unit analyses which show the number of items (content, activities, materials, and measuring devices) which are coded for each objective in a given unit. Another program can print out all the items stored for a single objective. Other combinations are limited only by the human imagination. Any of the 260 variables (in some cases there may be more or fewer) can be used as a criterion for item selection. For example, what curriculum suggestions exist for someone interested in folklore, or for a male student, or for a given reading level, or for any combination of variables about learners? Even professional variables can be used. For example, what suggestions exist for large-group instruction only or for display through visual devices, etc.? The potential for curriculum analysis as a basis for further development is extremely great.

Adapting the Data Base. Through the addition of new coding variables, the existing data base can be adapted to "special" education needs. One example of this is the addition of characteristics of students frequently classified for exceptional education. By recording existing units, they have been successfully used by many special education teachers throughout the United States. Other unique student populations could be accommodated in the same way, although the program emphasized individual differences, in general.

Media Utilization Studies. One proposal which at present is pending would attach a librarian and media specialist to coordinate efforts at selecting, locating, and acquiring instructional materials. Studies need to be conducted to analyze the effectiveness and quality of media, how they can best be provided for classroom use, and how they can best be utilized. The teacher needs to be as careful in his selection of instructional media as does the physician in the selection of medicine, and media utilization studies are necessary to provide data for making this selection.

Special Projects. These may cover a wide range of special interests. One such special project is analyzing a commercially produced television series not presently available for classroom use. Experts will divide the master tapes into "logical instructional sequences," and will specify the likely learning outcomes of these sequences and the student population characteristics for which they seem best suited. These will then be stored for use when the combination of objectives and learner characteristics for which they are suited are specified by a requesting teacher. Another special project has applied the program to the development of an individualized program of inservice education for secondary school principals. Again, the possibilities are immense and limited only by human imagination and ability.

Development

The second major component which may be part of this level of utilization is the creation of new units for the data base. Although several of the suggested service activities also involve development, there is a need for this as a distinct activity, though distinct from service in theory only because the relationship between service and development is, in reality, quite close.

This component should consist of the actual writing and coding of new units to be stored on magnetic tape or disc for computer retrieval. Ideally, this function should be an ongoing curriculum development activity. Further, some experts believe this function should be part of the normal duties of classroom teachers. In order to make this an integral, continuous operation, certain considerations must be given to providing the teacher with additional time, assistance, and compensation. Without these provisions, little success can be expected.

The development component could foster unique applications of computer assisted planning, as would the service component. Several additional possibilities may be suggested in the section on Implications found later in this chapter.

Third Level Utilization

Toward the more complex end of the hypothetical utilization continuum would appear a most comprehensive form of computer assisted planning. Since extensive preparation would be necessary to enter this phase, little will be said about it at this point. Those institutions wishing to become involved to this extent would have already passed through some other level and would be in a position to know of the specific kinds of activities in which they would be involved.

Essentially, this level would consist of becoming a major service center for a large geographical region, and becoming part of a proposed national network of computers. Harnack describes this proposal:

> *Developing a National Network of Computers.* As soon as computer usage increases, national networks of computers will be established. In fact, international networks will be established at the same time. When these networks exist, it will benefit teachers and students to such an extent and degree, that many professionals still cannot visualize what this will mean for the improvement of instruction. Paradoxically, such a national network will probably promote more diversity in the curriculum than it will promote similarity. Therefore, the bugaboo of a national curriculum, which of course is detrimental to education, would be overcome by a national network of computers because the teacher, in his own local office, would have access to and therefore more freedom to select from the suggestions, ideas, recommendations, and plans of thousands of teachers who have been active in the building of better learning environments for students. For retrieval purposes, the computer is nothing more than a wonderful tape recorder that remembers everything and can relate it to a thousand other things if told to do so. Therefore, tomorrow's teacher will have tremendous planning help because of the recorded teaching-learning suggestions from all other teachers, to say nothing of the suggestions of instructional materials at his disposal—literally, the resources of the world.[5]

Utilization Summary. There are innumerable ways in

which educators can employ computer assisted planning, its principles and procedures. Described above is a hypothetical continuum from the simple to the complex levels of utilization. Only three points on this continuum are described and many, many more levels and approaches are possible. However, for those interested in making the effort to apply the process, the continuum may be helpful in selecting a level at which to become involved. There has been no attempt to suggest that entry at a lower level is prerequisite to advancing to a more complex and comprehensive stage. However, becoming involved in utilization at the highest levels would certainly require experience with the application of computers to the process of planning for the individualization of instruction.

Implications

Just as with the many possible types of utilization, the infinite implications of computer assisted planning defy thorough description in this short space. Several of these implications have already been mentioned in the previous section and this section offers several more. Hopefully, the discussion presented here will be suggestive of many more possible applications and will stimulate others to explore this fertile field. There is no intended significance to the order in which these implications appear in this section. Where actual attempts have been made to utilize any of the potential applications in a practical situation, the work is referred to so that further information may be obtained if desired. The topics discussed are diagnosis of learner needs, monitoring pupil progress, monitoring the curriculum and instruction, inservice education, educational management, generation of new curriculum organization, research, and a network of computers.

Diagnosis of Learner Needs

An investigation is presently underway at the State University of New York at Buffalo to develop a system utilizing computers to diagnose the needs of learners for the specification of appropriate instructional objectives. At some time in the future this system will permit the direct communication of data about learners between the classroom and computer memory banks. For maximum convenience, it is hoped that this communication can be accomplished orally rather than through the modes possible with existing inter-facing between user and machine. The data to be so communicated will constitute a profile of each learner's background to include data on past achievements, interest, experiences, and anything else which will enable the accurate identification of individual needs. By coding objectives already stored in the computer memory banks to key words to be used to describe the diagnostic data, the computer will be able to suggest instructional objectives which are related to each unique learner profile.

Concomitant to the storage and use of diagnostic data, the computer memory would store data about learner characteristics such as is described in Chapter II for the purpose of screening instructional procedures to match them to individual students. At present these screens for selection are used but must be manually placed in the computer with each unit application. The use of the computer to store and automate this procedure of describing learner characteristics would save considerable time and effort for the classroom teacher and potential user of computer assisted planning.

Monitoring Pupil Progress

In like manner, data about pupil progress during and after the studying of selected objectives from a specific unit will be fed into the memory banks and will become part of the pupil profile. Instantly produced print-outs will provide an invaluable record and tool for diagnosis at all stages of instruction, much as medical records of a patient's progress provide data which permit physicians to make continuous judgments about the form of treatment being pursued, and about the patient's progress at getting well. Of course, wise utilization of these records of pupil progress will depend upon the ability of the teacher to make effective use of them. However, until such time that these services are available to teachers it is impossible to expect them to become trained in their use. In short, usage will improve through practice.

Monitoring Curriculum and Instruction

Again, in a similar manner, data will be kept on the effectiveness of the data bank of instructional suggestions, itself. Each time a use is made of a suggestion from the bank, evidence pertaining to its effectiveness and efficiency can be added to the "update files." When sufficient evidence warrants making changes in the data bank, the appropriate alterations can be quickly and easily entered into the system.

This particular monitoring system is presently in operation at one of the centers where the data banks are stored. Users of units may suggest alterations by telephone (on a 24-hour basis), by mail, or in person. These suggestions consist primarily of additions to the data already contained in the units but may also include recommendations to correct errors. Eventually, these suggestions will pertain to all aspects of the print-outs including the sequence of items suggested for a teaching-learning situation.

Inservice Education

Though hardly separable from other aspects of curriculum planning and instruction, there are definite implications inherent in computer assisted planning for the improvement of professional competencies. On one level, the use of computer assisted planning requires great skill on the part of teachers. Evidence (see Chapter IV) strongly suggests that the very use of these procedures facilitates improvements in instructional behavior. In short, when given an opportunity to make decisions about curriculum and instruction, most teachers will take whatever measures are necessary to make the best decisions. It is when there are no choices to be made that professionals become static in terms of self improvement. For example, what does a teacher have to know about instructional media when he is restricted to the use of a single textbook, often chosen by someone else? Given a wider range of choices in planning teaching-learning situations seems to encourage professional self improvement.

On another level of inservice education, computer assisted planning could be utilized to provide instructional suggestions for staff development. In other words, units could be written on topics related to teacher inservice education. From these units teachers could select objectives related to the attainment of specific instructional competencies. By selecting the objective and describing appropriate individual characteristics, the computer can provide the teacher with suggestions for attaining the objective. This differs little from the present use of computer assisted planning but, made convenient to the potential user by placing remote terminals in proper locations, the possibilities for self improvement are infinite. At present, an existing unit entitled "Individualizing Instruction" may have utility at this level of training, although it was originated for preservice education of teachers.

Educational Management

The same procedures as described above for inservice teacher education could be applied to most areas of educational management. For example, suppose a principal has a problem with class scheduling and wants to know more about better scheduling programs which might be applied to his school. This principal might select an objective related to reviewing available scheduling programs and then describe certain characteristics of his particular situation (student population, staff size, space available, etc.). The computer, in turn, can provide him with the information he needs relevant to his unique situation. There are few, if any, situations to which this could not be applied with proper programming of the computer and development of a data base.

Generation of Alternate Forms
of Curriculum Organization

All curricula are organized around certain unifying threads or themes. Sometimes these unifying threads are related primarily to student characteristics, sometimes to society, and sometimes to an academic discipline or combination of disciplines. Whatever the existing organizers are, through the kind of cross coding of items presently used, alternate organizers can be used to generate "new" curriculum programs. Harnack described one such application of this idea:

At this writing 35 computer-based resource units exist in the data file. All of these resource units have been coded to the same variables. If one now wishes to develop a new resource unit about a topic or theme which does not exist in the data file, but about which one can identify related variables, it is possible to generate a new resource unit from units already in existence. For example, recently the Center for Curriculum Planning at the State University of New York at Buffalo received a request for a resource unit on the *Humanities.* Since no such resource unit existed, the staff wrote a machine program which would extract from all of the existing resource units in the computers all of the objectives, content items, introductory, developmental, and culminating activities, instructional materials, and measuring devices related to the following variables: *Fine Arts, Humanities, Art, Folklore, Creating and Constructing, Drama, Poetry, Music and Creative Writing.* The result was a resource unit containing hundreds of items related to variables which were identified as relating to the Humanities. The important point is that the future development of specific resource units for a teacher who wants to explore a new center of interest may no longer be so laborious as before.[6]

It can be seen from this description that the use of key variables, and combinations of variables, can greatly enhance the flexibility of the curriculum. Certain ones can be specified to give special emphasis to some consideration such as small-group activities only, independent activities only, print or non-print materials only, any of a number of other variables, or combinations of variables. In addition, certain portions of the teaching-learning suggestions can be emphasized over others. For example, a teacher might wish to emphasize an "activity-based curriculum" and minimize the instructional content or materials as centers of focus. The alternatives for organizing the curriculum through the use of computer assisted planning are simply too numerous to be adequately described here; the possibilities described above barely begin to scratch the surface.

Research and Evaluation

The potential for research of computer assisted planning has been discussed in the previous chapter. The aspect which needs emphasis here is the utility of the program for facilitating curriculum study and analysis. Print-outs can be obtained which reveal many otherwise less obvious aspects of the curriculum. For example, item counts can be made showing the number of statements of content, activities, materials, and measuring devices for all the objectives stored in the memory bank. For further analysis, the computer could be programmed to print out the actual items for any or all of the objectives to reveal their exact nature. Also, the kinds of instructional objectives contained in the units can be easily examined. Of course, the point of these kinds of analyses would be to determine the effectiveness and efficiency of the curriculum and to identify areas of needed development.

Network of Computers

The value of linking major computer centers has also been discussed earlier. The resources of the entire world could be brought to bear on the planning of teaching-learning situations with amazing ease. Furthermore, if it has not already been recognized, it is now apparent that major improvements in instruction demand worldwide sharing of ideas which are successful.

Summary of Implications

The areas discussed above for which computer assisted planning has implications are far from a complete listing. These implications, in fact, should be considered merely suggestive of countless applications which have yet to be discovered. They are offered to give some general idea of how computer assisted planning might contribute to the ultimate goal of the school: to improve instruction so that learning can be best facilitated through assisting the decision making process.

Conclusion

This chapter attempts to conclude the task to which this book is addressed—bringing computer assisted planning to educators who may benefit most from its use. Mindful of Guba's advice that an invention must be diffused and adopted to be of real value, this final chapter aimed at providing much of the information necessary for utilization of some form of computer assisted planning of instruction.

The degree and kinds of adoption will vary from situation to situation. This chapter has attempted to conceptualize a continuum of applications from the relatively simple to the complex. Three points on this continuum have been described as illustrative of many possible variations. In particular, these range from the use of resource guides generated by computers at existing service centers, through the establishment of local service agencies with a development component, to the creation of a regional service agency as part of a network of such centers.

The numerous implications of computer assisted planning of instruction can hardly be described in so short a space as this book provides. The eight areas—diagnosis of learner needs, monitoring pupil progress, monitoring curriculum and instruction, inservice education, educational management, generation of alternate forms of curriculum organization, research and evaluation, and a network of computers—discussed in this chapter are no more than illustrative of countless more yet to be recognized. Viewed as suggestive only, and with increased awareness and utilization of the concept of using computers to help plan for instruction, these and many other possibilities may, indeed, become a reality.

References

1. Guba, Egon G. "The Process of Educational Improvement." Goulet, R.R. (ed.) *Educational Change: The Reality and the Promise.* New York: Citation Press, 1968.
2. *Ibid.*
3. Harnack, Robert S. *Computer-Based Resource Units in School Situations.* Buffalo: State University of New York at Buffalo, April, 1969, 22.
4. O'Connell, Joseph M. (ed.) *Evaluation of an Innovation in Education—Computer-Based Curriculum Planning.* Buffalo: State University of New York at Buffalo, February, 1970, 78, 81.
5. *Ibid.*
6. *Ibid.*

SUGGESTED READINGS

Original Study

Harnack, Robert S. "The Use of Electronic Computers to Improve Individualization of Instruction Through Unit Teaching." Buffalo, New York: State University of New York at Buffalo and Research Foundation of the State University of New York, Cooperative Research Project No. D-112, 1965.

Related Articles

Harnack, Robert S. "Computer-Based Resource Units." *Educational Leadership,* Vol. 23, No. 3, December, 1965, pp. 239-45.

Harnack, Robert S. "The Use of Electronic Computers to Improve Individualization of Instruction Through Unit Teaching." *Automated Education Letter,* Vol. 1, No. 5, February, 1966, pp. 3-8.

Harnack, Robert S. "Teacher Decision Making and Computer-Based Resource Units." *Audiovisual Instruction,* NEA, Vol. 12, No. 1, January, 1967, pp. 32-35.

Eisele, James E. and Harnack, Robert S. "Improving Teacher Decision Making and Individualization." *The Quarterly,* Western New York School Study Council, State University of New York at Buffalo, Vol. 18, No. 4, May, 1967.

Harnack, Robert S. "Resource Units and the Computer." *The High School Journal,* The University of North Carolina Press, Vol. 51, No. 2, December, 1967.

Eisele, James E. "Computers in Curriculum Planning." *Educational Technology,* Vol. 7, No. 22, November 30, 1967, pp. 9-16.

Harnack, Robert S. "Use of the Computer in Curriculum Planning." In special issue: "Uses and Values of the Computer in Education," edited by Richard Wolf. *International Review of Education,* UNESCO Institute for Education, Hamburg, Vol. 109, No. 2, 1968, pp. 154-169.

Eisele, James E. "Computers and the Process of Teacher Decision Making." *Impact,* Vol. 4, No. 2, Spring, 1969, pp. 27-35.

Center for Curriculum Planning. *Computer-Based Resource Units in School Situations,* Faculty of Educational

Studies, State University of New York at Buffalo, April, 1969.

Clayback, Thomas J. "Using Computers for Curriculum Planning and Research." *The Quarterly,* Western New York School Development Council, State University of New York at Buffalo, Vol. 21, No. 1, November, 1969.

Holden, George S. "The Effects of Computer-Based Resource Units Upon Instructional Behavior." *The Journal of Experimental Education,* Vol. 37, No. 3, Spring, 1969, pp. 27-30.

O'Connell, Joseph M. (ed.) *Evaluation of an Innovation in Education—Computer-Based Curriculum Planning.* State University of New York at Buffalo, February, 1970.

Research Studies
Hicken, James E. "An Experimental Analysis of the Effects on Pupil Achievement of Using an Electronic Computer in Individualizing Instruction Through Unit Teaching," Unpublished Doctoral Dissertation, State University of New York at Buffalo, 1965.

Goldberg, Minerva J. "Using a Resource Guide to Pre-Plan a Unit of Instruction," Unpublished Doctoral Dissertation, State University of New York at Buffalo, 1966.

Eisele, James E. "Using Resource Guides to Teach the Skills of Critical Thinking," Unpublished Doctoral Dissertation, State University of New York at Buffalo, 1966.

Holden, George S. "Changes in Instructional Behavior of Non-Unit Teaching Teachers When Resource Guides Are Used," Unpublished Doctoral Dissertation, State University of New York at Buffalo, 1967.

Licata, William J. "The Resource Guide as an Aid for the Teaching of Understanding," Unpublished Doctoral Dissertation, State University of New York at Buffalo, 1969.

Young, James H., Jr. "The Use of a Computer-Based Resource Guide to Pre-Plan a Unit of Instruction and to Develop Student Attitudes Toward Mathematics," Unpublished Doctoral Dissertation, State University of New York at Buffalo, 1970.

Wallingford, Ronald R. "Evaluation of an Application of a Computer Retrieval System for Exercise Physiology," Unpublished Doctoral Dissertation, State University of New York at Buffalo, 1970.

Davitt, Robert J. "Using Computer-Based Resource Guides to Teach the Skills of Listening," Unpublished Doctoral Dissertation, State University of New York at Buffalo, 1970.

Bianchi, Gordon B. "A Descriptive Comparison of the Differences Among Instructional Objectives Which Are Formulated and Selected With and Without the Participation of Students," Unpublished Doctoral Dissertation,

State University of New York at Buffalo, 1970.

McMahon, Edward James. "Using a Computer Generated Resource Guide to Plan for and Implement Individualization of Instruction in a Team Teaching Arrangement—A Descriptive Case Study," Unpublished Doctoral Dissertation, State University of New York at Buffalo, 1970.

McClarin, Robert L. "Valuing as a Dimension of the Educational Process," Unpublished Doctoral Dissertation, State University of New York at Buffalo, 1970.

Burr, Bruce D. "Student Participation in the Selection of Instructional Objectives," Unpublished Doctoral Dissertation, State University of New York at Buffalo, 1970.

APPENDIX A

REVISED OBJECTIVES—THE AMERICAN PEOPLE

This unit is designed around three main themes: immigration, world population explosion since World War II (including a study of women's rights and patterns of American culture), and an analysis of the movement for civil and political rights. Special emphasis has been accorded the civil rights movement in connection with the American Negro.

Affective

1.00 RECEIVING—None
2.00 RESPONDING—None

3.00   VALUING
    3.01   Acceptance of a Value
        (42)   To evaluate the reaction to citizens whose national origin is that of an enemy.
    3.02   Preference for a Value
        (46)   To evaluate the national origins quota system and/or the present immigration policy in terms of basic American principles.

4.00   ORGANIZATION—None
5.00   CHARACTERIZATION—None

Cognitive

1.00   KNOWLEDGE
    1.10   Knowledge of Specifics—None
    1.11   Knowledge of Terminology
        (1) To use correctly the following terms connected with the major theme of this unit (e.g., immigrant, migration, quota, national, alien, origins, displaced person, refugee, nativist, assimilation, acculturation, melting pot, and pluralistic).

        (126) To define terms relevant to the study of culture: acculturation, cultural diffusion, assimilation, discrimination, cultural pluralism, culturally deprived, social class, regionalism, patriarchal, matriarchal, egalitarian.

        (119) To identify clearly defined sub-cultures existing on a national level, e.g., Puerto Rican, Negro, American Indian, Mormons, and Amish.

        (143) To define the concept of civil rights.

1.12 Knowledge of Specific Facts

   (2) To identify the geographic location of the three great Indian Empires: the Incas, Aztecs, and Mayans.

   (3) To describe the conditions in which African Negroes were procured, shipped and received in America.

   (4) To label on an outline map of the world a minimum of four countries from which most immigrants came to America during the 18th and 19th centuries.

   (5) To list at least six European countries from which most immigrants came to the United States before 1930.

   (6) To identify the geographic regions of Europe from which the majority of immigrants came during the 19th century.

   (7) To identify the geographic regions of Europe from which the majority of immigrants came during the 20th century.

   (8) To explain two reasons why the majority of immigrants in the 20th century came from Southern and Eastern Europe.

   (10) To describe four economic conditions in America prior to 1890 which encouraged an unrestricted immigration policy.

   (11) To describe social, economic and political conditions which motivated people to leave their homes to settle in the English colonies.

   (64) To list the outstanding contributions to American society by at least five immigrant groups.

   (14) To describe social, economic and political

conditions which motivated people to leave their homes to settle in the United States during the 19th century.

(17) To describe social, economic and political conditions which motivated people to leave their homes to settle in the United States during the 20th century.

(20) To identify at least five personal traits of the immigrants which motivated them to come to the United States.

(22) To describe why the U.S. government admitted into the country at least three special groups of immigrants between 1929-1965 beyond quota limitations.

(26) To describe the special difficulties of at least four separate immigrant groups in gaining acceptance in American society.

(29) To describe the economic and social characteristics of an ethnic ghetto.

(35) To describe the kind of restrictions placed on immigrants in the 19th century by specific reference to pertinent legislation.

(28) To cite evidence proving that groups such as the Irish, Jews, Poles, Italians, Chinese, Japanese, and others had special difficulties in gaining or not gaining acceptance into the "American mainstream."

(75) To list several political gains of women since 1920.

(52) To identify three reasons why the contemporary American family is or is not a tightly woven unit.

(81) To list ways in which population growth affects the standard of living in the United

States.

(73) To describe the contributions of women's movements for women's rights.

(87) To identify three major changes in age group composition of American society from the Colonial Period to today.

(48) To identify factors which led to the dominant position of the male in Colonial Society.

(77) To give historical examples of factors controlling population growth in the past and present.

(103) To identify women's rights reform leaders in the fields of education, careers, and politics, during the 19th century.

(57) To identify the cultural patterns of age groups, in relation to interest outside their community, devotion to the past, and interest in the creative arts.

(49) To describe how the dominant position of the male in European societies had a great influence on the societal patterns from 1607 to 1850.

(105) To state the accomplishments in women's rights during the 19th century.

(50) To describe two prominent religious beliefs transplanted in America from Europe and at least two religious beliefs that originated in America.

(54) To identify the aspects of American culture which were derived from European culture and adapted to the needs or realities of American life.

(62) To cite evidence to show that the new

phenomenon of the teenage sub-culture transcends socio-economic levels as well as regional and national boundaries.

(98) To identify provisions for civil rights in the Northwest Ordinance of 1787.

(94) To identify historical examples of cases which have helped to bring about the following categories of civil rights: rights to self-expression, judicial rights, voting rights, employment rights, housing rights, and education rights.

(150) To list examples of court decisions and legislation which legally prevented the assimilation of Negroes into the mainstream of American culture in the 19th and 20th centuries.

(148) To list the major contributions of Negroes to the development of the American economy and culture during the 19th and 20th centuries.

1.20 Knowledge of Ways and Means of Dealing with Specifics.

(47) To compare present U.S. immigration policies with the immigration policies of another highly developed nation and an underdeveloped nation.

(21) To isolate, through the use of a case study, the economic, political and religious factors which were involved in the Irish immigration of the 19th century.

(23) To determine to what extent U.S. post-World War II immigration policy has resulted in a "brain drain."

(32) To contrast the positions taken in Emma

Lazarus' poem "The New Colossus" with Thomas Bailey Adrich's "Unguarded Gate."

(45) To contrast the Immigration Act of 1965 with the immigration policies adopted during the 1920's.

(56) To compare the American cultural patterns of urban and rural areas in relation to levels of sophistication, degree of homogeneity and interest in the creative arts.

1.21 Knowledge of Conventions—None.

1.22 Knowledge of Trends and Sequences.

(74) To trace the development of the women's rights movement from the Seneca Falls Convention to the passage of the 19th Amendment.

(58) To trace the growth of urban problems.

1.23 Knowledge of Classifications and Categories.

(55) To identify the various American cultural patterns that exist within geographical regions in the United States in relation to homogeneity of population, devotion to the past, and intergroup relations.

1.24 Knowledge of Criteria—None.

1.25 Knowledge of Methodology—None.

1.30 Knowledge of the Universals and Abstractions in a Field—None.

1.31 Knowledge of Principles and Generalizations—None.

1.32 Knowledge of Theories and Structures—None.

2.00 COMPREHENSION

2.10 Translation

(63) To explain at least one contribution of

several outstanding American immigrants.

2.20   Interpretation

(30) To explain why immigrants settled in ethnic ghettos.

(33) To explain reasons why native born Americans feared and opposed admittance and acceptance of immigrants.

(34) To explain nativist opposition to various immigrant groups.

(40) To explain reasons for legislation restricting immigration from nations which have been hostile toward the U.S.

(68) To explain the extent to which women control the wealth of the United States.

(130) To describe the impact of rapid cultural change on previously well-established institutions, e.g., church, government, schools.

(122) To explain the rise of the socio-economic independence of children in American society.

(85) To explain factors that have determined age distribution of our population since the Colonial Period.

(86) To explain, by citing some examples from certain periods in the development of American society, the close relationship between life expectancy at birth and labor supply.

(89) To explain, by citing examples in our present society, the close relationship between current age groups and changing needs in education.

(82) To explain how technological factors may

increase food supply.

(67) To explain the relevance of factors which have brought about change in women's work role such as availability of free education, wars, and apparent willingness to accept low pay.

(65) To demonstrate to what extent the characteristics of women's role in the European patriarchal society were retained as characteristics of woman's role in the Colonial Period.

(69) To compare the man's role and the woman's role in the United States before 1900 in relation to: legal rights, control and management of property, occupation, education, and political activities engaged in.

(83) To compare GNP, per capita income, and population figures for the years 1950 and 1960 for the U.S., India, Japan and Canada.

2.30 Extrapolation

(79) To list factors that should result in increased food supplies in the 20th century in the United States.

(88) To predict the social, political, and economic implications of the following statement: "Approximately half of the people in the United States are under the age of 25."

(91) To foretell future housing trends on the basis of current population age group studies.

(90) To predict future needs in education on

the basis of present population age groups.

(92) To predict needs for the aging on the basis of current age group analysis.

(124) To determine the effect religion, race, political institutions, and geography have on over-population.

(116) To conclude from careful study that legal, property, and employment rights of women vary from state to state.

3.00 APPLICATION

(66) To illustrate statistically that women's role in the labor force changed by mid 20th century as opposed to 1900.

(25) To apply the concept of acculturation to three groups of people, using specific examples such as language, customs, music, and employment.

4.00 ANALYSIS

4.10 Analysis of Elements

(84) To analyze the factors which impede solutions to the population problem.

(3) To analyze the conditions in which African Negroes were procured, shipped and received in America.

(102) To analyze the relationship between the 13th, 14th, 15th, and 24th Amendments to the federal Constitution and the civil rights of American Negroes.

(115) To compare the records of each Presidential administration since 1945 in the field of civil rights in terms of the types and amounts of activity for which they were largely responsible.

(149) To analyze the difficulties Negro migrants from the rural South experienced in adjusting to life in Northern urban centers.

(106) To differentiate the strategies used by leaders like Booker T. Washington, W.E.B. DuBois, and Marcus Garvey for promoting the civil rights of Negro Americans early in the 20th century.

4.20 Analysis of Relationships

(31) To analyze those conditions which prevented immigrants from leaving the ghetto.

(41) To analyze the role of the patriotic factor in the suppression of citizens whose national origin is that of the enemy nation by explaining its psychological utility to warfare.

(27) To analyze the rate of social mobility of immigrant groups in the United States with respect to residence, occupation, education, religion, and color.

(123) To analyze the relationship between age and restrictions placed on employment opportunities.

(125) To analyze ways in which society has reacted against cultural changes of the 20th century.

(118) To analyze the significance of the increase in divorce rate related to the American family unit.

(120) To analyze one effect that shifting population patterns have upon regional differences, e.g., east-west flow, rural-urban

flow.

(129) To analyze the impact of American culture on the cultures of other nations.

(59) To analyze shifting population trends from rural to urban to suburban areas from 1800 to 1960.

(76) To analyze the impact of technological change in the 19th century on the women's rights movement.

(80) To analyze the thesis that the United States government and state governments have a responsibility to make available birth control information.

(72) To analyze the relationship of education and the status of women in society.

(93) To analyze the relationships between shifting population patterns and the present urban crisis.

(97) To analyze the relationships between civil rights and the Declaration of Independence.

(95) To analyze the relationship between civil rights and the establishment of the English colonies.

(101) To compare legislation such as the citizenship rights of American Indians as they were defined by the Dawes Act of 1887, the Wheeler-Howard Act of 1924, and the Indian Reorganization Act of 1934.

(107) To analyze the relationships between the creation of separate economic and political instructions advocated by some black nationalist leaders' and Negroes' drive for equality.

(108) To analyze the relationships between the creation of separate economic and political institutions advocated by some black nationalist leaders' and Negroes' drive for equality.

(114) To compare the leadership assumed by the legislative and executive branches of the national government in promoting the civil rights of Negro Americans since 1945.

(112) To analyze the effects of the New Reconstructions on the civil rights of American Negroes.

(146) To contrast the family structures of white Americans and Negro American slaves.

(151) To contrast the goals of Jim Crow laws enacted at the beginning of the 20th century with civil rights legislation passed since 1957.

(142) To contrast living conditions on the voyages and the sale of labor on arrival of European and African immigrants to America in the 18th century.

4.30 Analysis of Organizational Principles—None.

5.00 SYNTHESIS

5.10 Production of a Unique Communication—None.

5.20 Production of a Plan, or Proposed Set of Operations.

(117) To propose an effective plan for preventing recurrences of the racial riots which have erupted in American urban centers since 1964.

(154) To propose effective remedies for the major civil rights problems confronting

Negro Americans in urban centers today.

5.30   Derivation of a Set of Abstract Relations

(9) To formulate an hypothesis about the immigration of the late 19th century and early 20th century as opposed to prior immigrations in terms of national origin.

(51) To formulate an hypothesis relating to the influence of one religious group in America from 1600-1750 that was manifested in the attitudes and actions of the people.

(53) To formulate an hypothesis relating to the apparent detachment of the family as a unit in mid-20th century United States as compared to the family as a unit in the mid-19th century.

(110) To formulate an hypothesis to explain the revolutionary character of programs sponsored by some black nationalist organizations for improving Negroes' position in American society.

(147) To formulate an hypothesis relating the economic plight of American Negro slaves to their social status.

6.00   Evaluation

6.10   Internal Criteria

(24) To evaluate by citing evidence for both of the following statements:

"The U.S. is the melting pot of the world."

"The U.S. is the salad bowl of the world."

(38) To evaluate the qualitative restrictions of the United States government from 1882 to 1920.

(39) To evaluate the quantitative restrictions of the United States government from the 1920's to the present.

(42) To evaluate the reaction to citizens whose national origin is that of an enemy.

(43) To evaluate the actions in time of war taken against citizens whose national origin is that of the enemy.

(44) To evaluate the immigration policies of the United States since the first administration of President Cleveland.

(46) To evaluate the national origins quota system and/or the present immigration policy in terms of basic American principles.

(128) To support or refute the hypothesis that there has been a cultural revolution in the 20th century in the United States.

(121) To test the hypothesis that there is a unique American character.

(152) To prove the hypothesis that "the Supreme Court has changed its mind on the issue of civil rights for Negro Americans" by contrasting its decisions in the cases of *Plessy vs. Ferguson,* 1896, and *Brown vs. Board of Education of Topeka, Kansas,* 1954.

(145) To evaluate the effects of slavery on the self-concept of American Negroes.

6.20 Judgments in Terms of External Criteria

(36) To evaluate the role of nativism throughout the history of America by examining the role of the "Know Nothings," "the Sandlot Riots," the Anti-Japanese move-

ment at the turn of the century, and the Ku Klux Klan.

(37) To evaluate the nativist movement in terms of basic American principles.

(70) To test the hypothesis that economic factors affect the role of women by examining the role of women on the plantation, on the frontier, and in the industrial north.

(60) To cite evidence to prove or disprove the statement: "Class distinctions are a thing of the past."

(61) To cite evidence to prove or disprove the statement: "Regionalism is a thing of the past."

(127) To evaluate the extent to which our rapidly changing culture is responsible for the generation gap.

(78) To evaluate the validity of the Malthusian theory of population pressure on limited natural resources in the United States.

(104) To evaluate the contributions of women's rights leaders to the attainment of their objectives.

(144) To analyze the thesis that Negroes had no civil rights prior to 1865.

(152) To prove the hypothesis that "the Supreme Court has changed its mind on the issue of civil rights for Negro Americans" by contrasting its decisions in the cases of *Plessy vs. Ferguson,* 1896, and *Brown vs. Board of Education of Topeka, Kansas,* 1954.

(100) To evaluate the extent to which the

Supreme Court enforces the Bill of Rights.

(99) To evaluate the extent to which the Bill of Rights insures civil rights.

(96) To evaluate the extent to which Colonial governments protected, promoted, and/or impeded civil rights.

(113) To evaluate the validity of the hypothesis that the New Reconstruction era began with the Supreme Court decision of 1954.

(111) To evaluate the extent to which racial violence—planned and spontaneous—has aided or hindered the civil rights movement in the 20th century.

(109) To evaluate the various strategies of Negro leaders and organizations for improvement in the Negro's position in America since 1900.

(153) To evaluate the effectiveness of various actions designed to promote the civil rights of American Negroes in the 20th century.

(145) To evaluate the effects of slavery on the self-concept of American Negroes.

APPENDIX B

LISTING OF CURRENTLY AVAILABLE UNITS

COMPUTER-BASED RESOURCE UNITS

Topic	Approximate Grade Level	Subject
Air Pollution	7	Science
American Civilization in Historic Perspective	11	Social Studies
American Cultural Revolution in the 20th Century	10-12	Social Studies
American People (The)	11	Social Studies
Communications	3	Social Studies
Communities of Man (The)	K-6	Social Studies
Conservation of Natural Resources	3-6	Science
Drugs and Narcotics	7-9	Health
Foods	3	Social Studies
Going To and From School	ages 6-12	Special Education
Human Growth and Development	K-9	Health
Individualization of Instruction	College	Teacher Education
Job Interview	7-12	Social Studies
Man and His Culture	4-6	Social Studies
Manifest Destiny	10	Social Studies
Market Place (The)	1-3	Social Studies
Measurement	3-8	Mathematics—Science
Movigenics	ages 6-9	Special Education
News Media Analysis	4-6	Language Arts
Physiology of Exercise	College	Physical Education
Quadratic and Trigonometric Functions	9	Mathematics
Sex Education	College	Health
Smoking	4-6	Health
Solar System and Beyond	1-6	Science
Speaking and Listening	1-6	Language
Transportation	3	Social Studies
Transportation's Influence on U.S. Development	11-12	Social Studies
United States Constitution	11	Social Studies
World War II	11	Social Studies